Benjamin De Costa

# The hand-book of Mount Desert, coast of Maine

With all the routes thither

Benjamin De Costa

**The hand-book of Mount Desert, coast of Maine**
*With all the routes thither*

ISBN/EAN: 9783337145781

Printed in Europe, USA, Canada, Australia, Japan

Cover: Foto ©Andreas Hilbeck / pixelio.de

More available books at **www.hansebooks.com**

# THE HAND-BOOK

OF

# MOUNT DESERT

## COAST OF MAINE

With all the Routes thither, Descriptions of the
Scenery and Topography, Sketches of the
History, with Illustrations and a Map
of Mount Desert, and Penobscot
and Frenchman's Bay, from the

## UNITED STATES COAST SURVEY.

An Island full of hills and dells,
All rumpled and uneven.
BROWNING.

BOSTON:
A. WILLIAMS & COMPANY.

NEW YORK:
T. WHITTAKER, 2 BIBLE HOUSE.

BAR HARBOR, ME.:
A. W. BEE.

# THE GUIDE TO MOUNT DESERT.

THE route to Mount Desert is one of the most enjoyable in the country, between Boston and Portland, the tourist being able to stop and make so
many delightful side excursions, like those to the
Isles of Shoals, the Beaches of New Hampshire and Maine,
and the resorts in Portland Harbor, for which see the
" Atlantic Coast Guide." But our starting-point is Portland
now.

At present there are two prominent routes by which the
tourist may reach Mount Desert: the Portland, Bangor and
Machias Line, and the Rockland, Mount Desert and Sullivan
steamers, starting respectively from Portland and Rockland.
The latter is preferred by those who would avoid a night at
sea and rough water, as the whole trip can be made in the
daytime. Tourists may buy tickets to go by one line and
return by the other. The scenery on the two routes is unlike.

Those who must avoid the water altogether take the rail-
road to Bangor, and go thence by the stage-coach or private
conveyance *via* Ellsworth and Trenton. Usually there is a
daily stage. The route is uninteresting, except the point

where, before reaching the low flat lands of Trenton, a view of Mount Desert and its environs is had.    The road passes over Trenton Bridge, which spans the Narrows.    The tourist is then in the Town of " Mount Desert," one of the three towns of the island, Eden being on the east side and Tremont on the south-west.

THE ROCKLAND ROUTE.—There are three ways of reaching Rockland, the last of which is the long night route by water, not generally recommended.

Route 1.—From Boston to Portland by rail, and stop over night.    Take the early train from Portland on the Maine Central *via* Brunswick, Bath, Knox & Lincoln R. R., arriving in Rockland at 11 A.M., where the cars are run to the steamer's wharf.

Route 2.—The above may be varied by taking the boat from Boston to Portland at 7 P.M., arriving in Portland at 5 A.M., in season for the early train to Rockland.

Route 3.—Take the Bangor steamers from Boston, Wednesdays and Fridays at 5 P.M., arriving in Rockland at 6 A.M., allowing time to get breakfast at a hotel before taking the Mount Desert steamer.

The steamer leaves Rockland, Tuesdays, Thursdays and Saturdays, on arrival of the train from the West, usually about 11 A.M.    Passing Owl's Head Light on the right hand we take an easterly course across Penobscot Bay.    To the north-west the Camden Hills rise above the waters of the bay, and make a fine appearance.    These hills were sketched by the pilot of the Popham Expedition in 1607, and have played their part in historical discussion.    We next approach Fox Island, once abundant in silver-gray foxes.    Here the British built a fort in 1779, and drove away the people.    The steamer passes the Fiddler Beacon, a square granite monument, marking a dangerous ledge at the entrance to the Thoroughfare.    On the right is Brown Head Light, passing which we enter the Thoroughfare and pass on to North Haven, where a boat takes off passengers. In leaving Fox Islands, we veer to the north, passing through the Little Thoroughfare, a smoother and shorter channel than the main one, and enter Isle au Haut Bay. Isle au Haut is seen rising 600 feet to the south-east. It was so called by Champlain. August 17, 1814, the sloop-of-war *John Adams*, 24 guns, went ashore here with sixty English prisoners, but afterwards got off and was burned to prevent her from falling into the hands of the British. First, however, we approach Deer Island on the south side, entering the Thoroughfare, and stop at Green's Landing, where a boat lands passengers.

These Thoroughfares are so called, for the reason that the numerous vessels plying up and down the coast generally go " through the land." In good weather the tourist will see hundreds of sails dotting the water, while during adverse winds the harbors are full of vessels. The scene is very animated. Great Deer Island is ten miles long, north and south, the centre having the form of a saddle. With Little Deer Island it forms the township of "Deer Isle." It abounds in granite, of which many of our public edifices are built, and is forested with derricks. The coast here is a vast bed of granite and the numberless islands through which the steamer winds, form exquisite scenery by the contrast between the bare granite ledges and the intense green of the pines and spruces with which the larger islands are covered. Occasionally a clump of islands appear to be one, but the clump gradually breaks up, and you sail on and on

> " Till each, retiring, claims to be
> An islet in an inland sea."

About ten miles from Deer Isle we pass through York's Narrows, and here have our first good view of Mount Desert.

Approached from this side, Western Mountain, rising grandly to the clouds, conceals the view of the rest of the chain, but as we near Bass Harbor Head the separate peaks gradually unfold, and, as the steamer rounds Long Ledge, they lie spread before us in a landscape rarely equalled in grandeur and beauty. On the left is Western Mountain, the East and West Peaks being plainly distinguished from here; next is Beech Mountain, then Dog and Robinson's Mountains, which together with Flying Mountain, form the western slope to Somes' Sound. Across the Sound is Mount Mansell, or Brown's Mountain, as it is sometimes called.

East of Mount Mansell, and rising far above in several distinct peaks, lies Sargent's Mountain, a vast rugged mountain over 1,300 feet in height. Next is Pemetic Mountain, so called from the Indian name of Mount Desert.

Then comes Green Mountain, easily distinguished by the little hotel on its summit. The highest of the range, it partially hides Dry Mountain. Last, Newport stands out well defined. On our right lie the Cranberry Islands. Passing these we turn to the left, and make our first landing at South-west Harbor about 3 P.M.

South-west Harbor is the oldest settlement on the Island, and is now widely known as the port where the Cimbria lay exciting so much curiosity, besides gratifying the trading propensities of the inhabitants by the money put in circulation.

The principal hotel is the Island House. Board can also be obtained in private families. South-west Harbor is a point whence the tourist can easily reach many of the finest views, being situated practically in the heart of the island. The resorts around the Harbor should be visited under favorable circumstances, like those at Bar Harbor. In fact, many a tourist, after a hasty and ill-timed visit to both Bar and South-west Harbors, has been heard to say, " There was nothing to see," and has expressed surprise that any one should care for Mount Desert at all.    As we aim to do justice to every part, the Editor may be permitted to make an observation with reference to the misapprehension that all the fine scenery is confined to one locality.  The southern side of this wonderful isle has attractions, which, while different, are not inferior to those found elsewhere, and in the immediate vicinity of South-west Harbor, the tourist, by the aid of our Hand-book, will find a great variety of extended and impressive views, together with a multitude of lesser scenes, that will linger in memory for life.   The visitor must spend more than one summer in the island, if he would gain any tolerable acquaintance with its charms.

Leaving South-west Harbor, Somes' Sound opens for a moment directly north, and the tourist should not fail to see the grand view presented by the precipitous sides of Dog Mountain, Robinson's Mountain, and Mount Mansell, while between the last two lie the "Narrows."   It was in Somes' Sound that Henry Hudson anchored his little vessel, the " Half Moon," in 1609, when on his way south to explore the Hudson River, which was *discovered* in 1524–5, and *mapped* in 1529.   Here Hudson delayed some time, and cut a new foremast.   Here, also, to possess himself of the peltry of the savages, he attacked them with cannon and musketry.   He probably landed not far from Fernald's Point, where the Jesuits attempted a colony in 1613.   This episode has escaped notice, but the cruel conduct of Hudson bore fruit in after times.   This is, perhaps, the first and last time that Dutch cannon ever resounded in Somes' Sound, where Argall's guns were heard four years later.   The French occupation was quite as brief as the Dutch.   No writer entitled to be heard on this point has ever taught that the Jesuits were here any four or five years, as often stated.

As we pass on, Greening's Island closes up the view of the

Sound for a time. The Sound is described in Chapter V. After a glimpse of Dog Mountain we pass North-east Harbor and Bear Island. Next is Seal Harbor, and now we approach some of the most frequented resorts of visitors. Otter Cove, a deep inlet with a high promontory on the east, rounding which we see Otter Cliffs, and at the bottom of a cove, formed by Great Head on the east, are the yellow sands of Newport Beach. Passing the frowning Great Head. Frenchman's Bay is before us, Egg Rock, with light-house and bell-tower, being the nearest island ; then beyond the bay the steep cliffs of Ironbound, while the bristling Porcupines stretch across from Mount Desert to Gouldsborough. On the left we see Schooner Head, and, just before reaching it, Anemone Cave. On the Head is a mass of white rock, which, seen at a distance, forms a good representation of a schooner under sail. (See pp. 132–8.)

The view of Newport is especially fine at this point, as the shadows give a depth to the landscape, which greatly enhances its richness. At Otter Creek Cliffs, persons with a good imagination can see the "Castle," with its battlements and windows.

The little "Thrumbcap" is soon passed. This is sometimes called the "Thumbcap." The island takes its name, however, from its resemblance to a cap decorated with "Thrums" or "Thrumbs," otherwise with tassels. The trees formed the tufts, or thrumbs. Quarles asks, "Are we born to thrumb caps?" There is no reference to "thumb-cap" or thimble. Next is the large island called the "Burnt Porcupine," or "Wheeler's" and "Fremont's" Porcupine. Now the cottages on Ogden's Point appear. Soon Bar Harbor is before us, and the tourist is agreeably surprised by the extreme beauty of the view, being so different from anything previously seen. Rounding Veazie's Point, about 4 P.M., we are at a crowded, noisy wharf.

Bar Harbor is the largest and most frequented of the many villages of Mount Desert. Numerous cottages hide themselves among the hills, or appear clustered along the shores, while every year large additions to its hotels are made. One '' boon '' is here vouchsafed to the weary tourist, the tuneful mosquito is unknown.

At the head of the landing is the Rockaway House with its pleasant piazzas, overlooking the bay. Turning to the right we reach the main avenue, and follow it up the ascent. On the right is the old Agamont, now unoccupied To the left is the Newport House, and, on the same side, the Ocean and Deering. Below these are a number of private cottages. Next on the right is the Rodick House, which, with its cottages, will probably accommodate more guests than any other hotel here. Near by is the store of E. G. Desisle, who keeps, as is usual in the country, well nigh everything; he is also Postmaster. Opposite the Rodick House is the Summer Establishment of Albert W. Bee, *Sole Agent* for Bailey's Boston Candies, and where the leading Boston and New York dailies are for sale and on file. The next hotel on the right is the Grand Central. On the left, at a short distance from the avenue, is the Atlantic House, a pleasant, quiet hotel, surrounded by cottages and having a fine view. Turning into the road leading to the Reservoir, we come to the Union Church, and the Public Library. The latter is supported by contributions of books from the summer visitors. Next is the Protestant Episcopal Church, a neat stone structure, built in 1877. A little farther, on the same side, is the St. Sauveur House, a name applied by the French in 1613 to their first landing place. The view from here is very fine. Next are the Lynam Cottages, and opposite is the elegant summer residence of Miss Shannon. Further still is the Belmont House. A short distance beyond is the Reservoir which supplies Bar Harbor with water.

On leaving the wharf, by the shore road, we pass the
floating stage, for row or sail-boats, and the Bowling Alley;
under which is a bathing establishment, with hot and cold,
fresh and salt water baths.    Farther on is the Hayward
House, beautifully located in one of the coolest spots.

But we must leave Bar Harbor and go on with the steamer
which passes between Bar Island and Sheep Porcupine, following the shore of Mount Desert westerly, landing at Lamoine,
and connecting with the stage for Ellsworth, 10 miles.   A fine
view of Mount Desert Narrows is obtained here, and the
*Ovens* can be seen on the Mount Desert shore.    Running
eastward, and after stopping at Hancock, we soon reach
Sullivan, the terminus.    Here is the Waukeag House, a new
and well-fitted hotel, accommodating over 200 guests, and
the tourist should spend a few days here, as the view of
Mount Desert from this point is fine, while the lakes and
streams abound with trout.

Returning, the steamer leaves Sullivan early, Mondays,
Wednesdays and Fridays, touching at Hancock and Lamoine,
and leaves Bar Harbor at 7 A.M., South-west Harbor 8.15
A.M., passing over the same route and arriving at Rockland
to connect with the 1 P.M. train for Portland, reached at 5.30
P.M., and connecting at the Transfer station with the P. & O.
R. R. for the White Mountains.   The train reaches North Con-
way at about 8 P.M.   Otherwise, proceeding direct to Boston,
the tourist arrives there at 9.30 P.M., in time for the Shore
Line Express to New York at 10 P.M., a sure connection.

The Portland Route.    This is the "Outside" route.
Take the evening train from Boston to Portland, Tuesdays
and Fridays, connecting with the steamer leaving Portland
11 P.M., reaching Rockland about 6 A.M., where connections
are made with the Sanford steamers leaving Boston at 5 P.M.

the previous evening. The steamer passes places of historic interest on the way to Portland, such as Pemaquid and Monhegan. For a full description of Penobscot Bay, in connection with this route, the reader is referred to the "Atlantic Coast Guide," furnished by the publishers of this book. The course taken by this route is more northerly, not going through the Thoroughfare, but keeping close to Long Island, 11¼ by ¼ miles, and forming a part of Ilesborough. The first point reached is Castine, a very ancient place once possessed by the French, and the scene of various encounters between them and the English. It is a charming place. The name calls up Baron Castine, of St. Castine, who, as the rhyme goes,

> "Has left his chateau in the Pyrenees,
> And sailed across the Western seas."

At one time an officer in the body-guard of the King of France, he was nevertheless of a romantic disposition, and in 1665, found his way to Quebec. Soon he reached this place, previously occupied by D'Aulney and Temple. For a quarter of a century he lived in his fort, having married the daughter of the Chief "Madackawando." He was at last driven out by Gov. Andross, when, in 1688, he anchored the Frigate Rose in front of the Fort, the site of which is still shown. In 1648, the Capuchins founded a house here. An United States fort now floats the stars and stripes. Leaving Castine, the steamer descends around Cape Rosier, enters Egemoggin Reach, a narrow strait between Deer Isle and the main, and lands at North Deer Isle. Thence we go across the Reach to Sedgwick. Leaving this place, the steamer emerges from the Reach and enters Blue Hill Bay. The scenery of the Reach is very inviting, and the tourist will see various pleasant spots that have a future in store. Champlain was familiar with this charming region. In describing it he says :

" Coming to the south of the High Island (Isle au Haut) and coasting it about one-fourth of a league, where there are several sand bars out of water, we turned to the west till we opened the mountains, which are to the north of said island. You can be assured that in seeing the eight or nine notches in the Isle of Mount Desert, . . you will not see any more islands." He says again that these mountains are " very high and notched, appearing from the sea like what seems to be seven or eight mountains on a line with each other and the tops of the most of them are without trees because all is rocks. I named it the Island of the Desert Mountain (*iles Mont desert*)." He thus intended to characterize the *mountains*, not the *island*, as desert, a point that has been overlooked in the discussion of the name, which, too, should have the accent where the French put it. From Blue Hill Bay, the view is grand, being similar to that had on the Rockland boat. Seaward will be noticed Burnt Coat or Swan's Island, which is rough and indented like the entire coast. Verrazano, the Italian, in the service of Francis I., compared it, as he sailed along, to the coast of Illyria and Dalmatia. Upon this island, a Mr. Swan built an elegant house, but gave up his place, which finally disappeared. It was Swan's " Folly." We next steam on to Bass Harbor Head, where the two routes are the same ; and for the description the reader will return to the Rockland route. We reach South-west Harbor about 2.30 P.M. Thence this line runs eastward to Millbridge, Jonesport, and Machiasport. A full description of this portion of the route will be found in the "Atlantic Coast Guide."

Returning by this route, the steamer leaves Bar Harbor about 10 A.M., Mondays and Thursdays ; South-west Harbor 11.30 A.M., arriving in Rockland 6 P.M., where connections are usually made with the Sanford line for Boston direct. Continuing, the steamer arrives in Portland, 1 A.M., connecting with the night train on the Eastern R. R. arriving in Boston, 6 A.M.

In arranging excursions from either Bar or South-west Harbor, the distances can be measured accurately on the map. The various resorts are grouped together in their respective classes, and, to find the account of any one, it will be necessary simply to turn to the chapter which includes its class. The map of the island given in this guide is absolutely correct, giving every road, pond, lake, and brook. The twenty-two mile drive is the great drive for a day, but it may be made a hundred and twenty-two and changed to a week.

Tourists are referred to the advertising pages for full information concerning hotels, routes, etc., and are assured that no pains will be spared to have the hand-book *correct* in *every* particular, and to make it an invaluable guide to all who would visit Mount Desert. We are indebted to *Harper's Magazine* for the sketches composing the frontispiece, except the view of Eagle Lake, which, by the courtesy of D. Appleton & Co., is from *Picturesque America.* Suggestions and any information desirable for the Guide may be sent to Albert W. Bee, who, either at Bar Harbor or 169 Tremont Street, Boston, will be happy to give freely any information desired by tourists. We are under great obligations to the officers of the United States Coast Survey for information and assistance so liberally given.

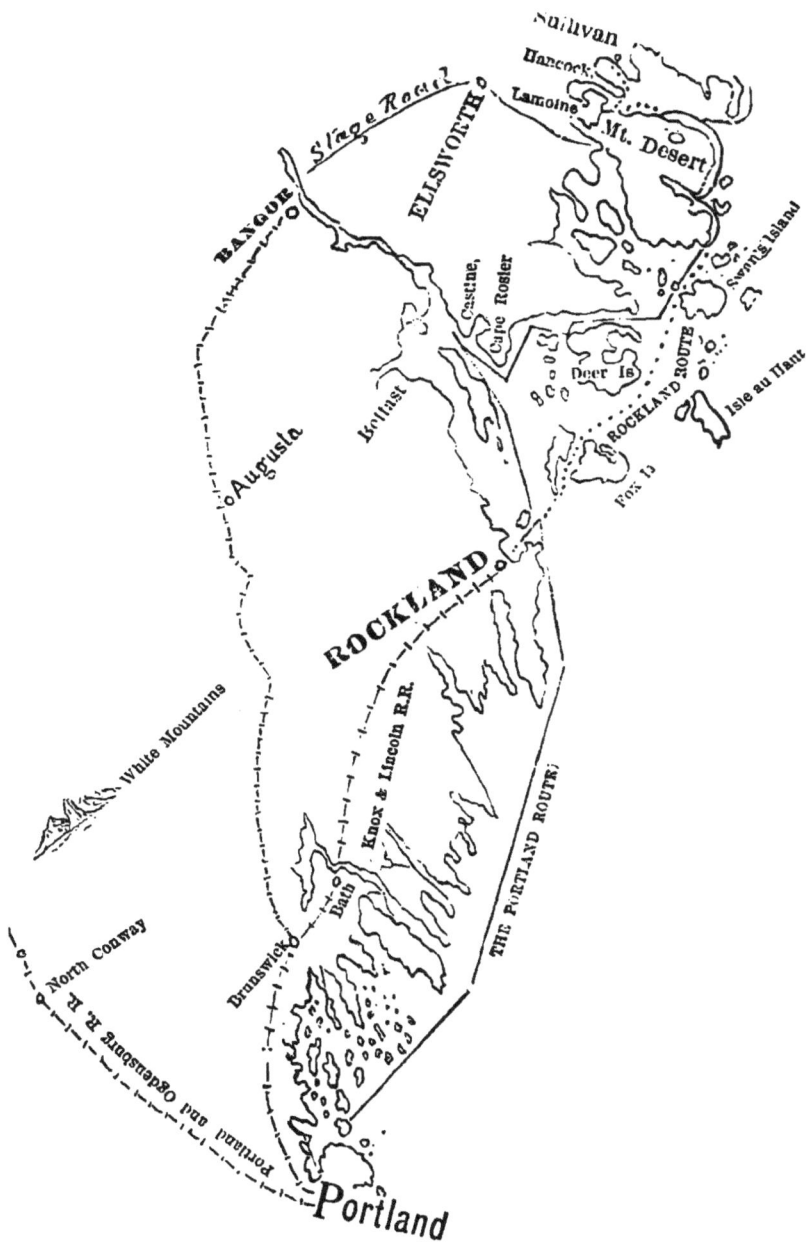

# CONTENTS.

# Mount Desert.

*BIRD'S-EYE VIEWS.*

## CHAPTER I.

THE COAST — ITS BEAUTIES — ITS PECULIARITIES — ITS
RIVERS — THE NORTHMEN — CABOT — VERRAZZANO —
GOSNOLD—PRING—DE MONTS—WEYMOUTH—POPHAM—
HENRY HUDSON — THE JESUITS.

EVERAL summers ago we were sitting
at an open window, looking out upon
one of the pleasant parks of New York,
vainly endeavoring to detect some per-
ceptible motion among the tall maples whose leaves
had hung ever since morning as immovable as foliage
cut in cold stone. But not a bough waved nor a leaf
stirred, for the dog-days had set in, and a Canicula
of unequalled intensity seemed fairly to weigh down
the whole world. It was almost impossible to breathe,
and the very grasshopper was a burden. Under the
circumstances, the mind recurred to every conceivable
refuge, and was tantalized by visions of far-off isles,
sown like gems in the sea, where, as the bard of Scio
imagined, the shrilly-breathing Zephyrus was ever

piping for the refreshment of man. At last fancy found expression in words, and we fell into a serious discussion of the merits of ocean and shore, and resolved to get out of the suffocating city without delay. But where should we go? Of course, repetitions of New York were suggested; and yet what real advantage should we find in any change that gave no fresh mental and moral air? The sickly dilutions of Long Branch would not suffice. And so (I hardly know how it came about) *Maine* was talked of. But what was there in Maine? We certainly did not want to go to Moosehead Lake at this season, to be devoured by black flies. Why, of course, there was " Mount Desert." The name was a novelty, and reminded us of the scenes which suggested the story of " The Pearl of Orr's Island." We at once looked up the place, and found, in several books of travel, brief references, by out-of-the-way tourists, to a wonderful isle off Penobscot Bay, an isle seen in early times[1] by sailors,

(1)—Many into whose hands this book may fall, will doubtless be glad to have here a few additional items on the early history of Maine, which are therefore given in the form of notes, to be skipped by the general reader. First, it must be observed that the pre-Columbian discovery of America is now regarded as an established fact. The authenticity of the Icelandic histories has been amply vindicated, and it is clear that the Atlantic Coast lying above the forty-first parallel was more or less familiar to the Icelandic navigators. Yet the shores of Maine are not mentioned in any of the Sagas. The principal voyages of which we have historical accounts were made to a locality called *Hop*, near the southeastern part of Massachusetts, for which place they laid their course when leaving the headlands of Nova Scotia. Consequently, while the shores of Labrador and Nova Scotia are delineated with considerable minuteness, nothing appears to apply to the coast of Maine.

Biarne, son of Heriulf, who was driven upon the American coast in the

and which was called " Mount Desert." It was a
perfect *terra incognita* to our minds ; but we at once
resolved on an exploration.   From Williamson's unre-
liable and yet invaluable book on Maine, we learned

year 985, doubtless saw this part of the country, and the early voyagers
probably came thither in their expeditions to obtain timber ; but the history
of Maine was nevertheless almost a blank as late as the beginning of the sixteenth century. About five years after the re-discovery of America by
Columbus, the Cabot brothers sailed southward along the coast of Maine,
though without leaving any memorial. In 1504 the Biscay fishermen are
known to have frequented the neighboring seas ; while in 1524 Verrazzano
coasted these romantic shores, being followed the next year by Stephen
Gomez, who in the course of this voyage became acquainted with the Hudson River, naming it River of St. Anthony. Among others who visited this
region about this period was the Frenchman John Alfonsce, a pilot of
Roberval. About the year 1542 he sailed south, and found a great bay in
latitude 42° N., which, in all probability, was Massachusetts Bay. A copy of
his map of the coast, made from the original, is in the possession of the
writer, for whom it was made by M. Davezac. But when we come down to
1602, Gosnold gives us more definite descriptions.

This navigator sailed from Falmouth, England, March 26, came in sight
of the coast of Maine May 4, in about the 43d degree of north latitude. The
land seen by him may have been Agamenticus, though some persons offer the
opinion that it was Mount Desert. In this region Gosnold met eight Indians
in a shallop, which they probably had obtained of some Biscay fishermen.

June 7, the year following, Martin Pring came in sight of the coast, and
afterwards explored the entire seaboard. The accounts which he gave on
his return were reliable and exact.

In the winter of 1604–5, De Monts with his party, who came from France
in the preceding May, lived on an island in the St. Croix River. In the
spring, De Monts, attended by Champlain and other gentlemen, coasted
southward in a small vessel, erecting a cross at the Kennebec, and taking
formal possession of the territory in the name of the King of France ; notwithstanding the voyage of Pring, according to the views of that age, gave
to the English Crown a prior right, Champlain went as far south as Cape
Cod, where he was wounded in a fight with the Indians. The map of the coast
drawn by him was the most exact of any hitherto made ; still it was sufficiently obscure.

In May of the same year, George Weymouth came out with an expedition
under the patronage of the Earl of Southampton, the friend of Shakespeare

something of the general features of the whole coast, and decided to take all the principal points on the way from the Isles of Shoals off Portsmouth Harbor, to

and on the seventeenth of the month reached an island on the coast, which he called St. George. This island was probably Monhegan. He afterwards explored the country, and then returned to England, carrying with him several Indians whom he kidnapped for the purpose.

In 1607 George Popham attempted to found a colony at Sagadahoc, where a fort and various buildings were erected. His first thought was to commence his colony on Stage Island, but he afterwards removed to the peninsula. It is claimed, though with no very strong reasons, that this was the first attempt to colonize the coast of Maine. But in all such claims local pride is liable to overreach itself. This colony at Sagadahoc was composed chiefly of persons more or less attached to the Church of England. They brought their chaplain with them, and held Divine Service here on the coast of New England, thirteen years before the Plymouth Pilgrims landed on the shores of Cape Cod. As is well known, after making a fair beginning, they were obliged to give up the enterprise and return to England. Thus it will be seen that popular notion, which makes the Plymouth Pilgrims the pioneers on an unknown coast, has little support in fact. The coast for nearly a hundred years had been tolerably well known, while they fell upon it by mistake, having originally laid their course for the Hudson River.

The history of the Maine coast is yet to be written by some person possessing ampler materials than are yet in hand, and with broader sympathies than any heretofore displayed.

The colony established in 1604-5 by De Monts, at Port Royal, was abandoned, but in 1611 it was re-established by Poutrincourt, who brought over Father Pierre Biard, a Jesuit Professor of Theology at Lyons, and Father Masse. The next year the Marchioness de Guercheville, the warm friend and patron of the mission, induced De Monts to surrender his patent, when it was conferred upon her by Louis XIII., who added all the territory in America between the St. Lawrence and Florida, with the exception of Port Royal, which had been previously confirmed to Poutrincourt. In 1613 the Marchioness prepared to take full possession of her territory in America. Le Saussaye commanded the ship that was sent out, and with him went Fathers Quentin and Lallemant, and Brother du Thet. Arriving at Port Royal, they found Fathers Biard and Masse. A very short time afterwards they left Port Royal in the "Honfleur," to establish a colony at Mount Desert. This was eleven years after Gosnold began his settlement at Cuttyhunk, and seven years before the Pilgrims landed at Plymouth.

Grand Menan, another isle of wonders, lying in the mouth of the Bay of Fundy.

Organizing our small force, we started for Boston, from whence we finally reached the famous Isles of Shoals, which glitter in the sea in sight of Rye (New Hampshire) Beach. At the " Shoals " we fairly commenced our tour, though in the plan of this book the description of this place is now omitted. But, before proceeding any further, we wish to say something definite in favor of Maine.

Now we know that that which is dearly bought is highly prized; and hence scenes viewed when travelling afar are esteemed above those found nigh at hand. Tourists flock annually to the Old World in search of natural beauties, as if there were nothing in our own land to excite admiration. And yet we have every variety of mountain and coast scenery, equal, if not superior, to that of foreign countries, almost within sight of all our doors.

We hear much, for instance, of the coast-scenery of Cornwall, the Isle of Wight, and the Mediterranean, but still we do not fear to place in comparison the varied and romantic beauties of the coast of Maine. The entire seaboard is fretted and fringed in the most remarkable manner, forming a long-drawn labyrinth of capes, bays, headlands, and isles. The mingling of land and water *is* indeed admirable. Here a cape, clad in pine greenery, extends out into the sea, coquettishly encircling a great field of blue waves; there a bold headland, with its outlying drongs, meets and buffets the billows with catapultic force; here the bright fiord runs merrily up into the land, the hills stepping down to its borders, mirroring their outlines as in a glass; there a hundred isles are sown, like sparkling emeralds, in the summer sea.

We need not plunge into the wild interior of Maine, and wander amid its mountains and lakes and streams, in order to discover a wealth of beauty. All that one can reasonably desire is found on the border. Sailing northward, the shores of the Atlantic are found comparatively uninteresting until we approach the coast of Maine, when all tameness vanishes, and the shore puts on a bold, rugged beauty that could hardly be surpassed.

Whoever carefully examines a good map of the continents will perceive that, in a multitude of cases, amounting almost to a general rule, the capes point southward, and that groups of islands are found south of the land. Or otherwise, that, as we proceed southward, we find the land tapering away and terminating in islands. This we have seen is eminently true of the coast of Maine. To account for the present configuration of this coast is extremely difficult. It looks as if its shores had been broken and serrated by glaciers, which, as Agassiz tells us, once covered the entire State. Before the retreat of the ice period, those vast glaciers, slowly descending from the mountains to the sea, might perhaps, in long ages, have thus ploughed out portions of the shores, forming capes and bays; yet we must in many cases account, for the islands at least, by other causes. Some are clearly the result of upheaval, while others may have been formed by the sinking of neighboring land beneath the surface of the waves. Yet, however this may be, the coast of Maine presents an appearance similar to what the Duke of Bourbon called, "that nook-shotten isle of Albion." And from its broken outline comes its beauty.

And it will be the aim of the writer in the present work to do something like justice to this really remarkable region, which is one that in the course of time must be very widely known and thoroughly appreciated by that rapidly increasing class who delight in all the varied and wayward moods of Nature, so splendidly illustrated among the mountains and along the shores between the Isles of Shoals and Grand Menan.

As regards the accommodations for travel, comparatively little has been said, though they will be found quite ample. They are subject to more or less change from season to season, and are at the same time improving. New resorts are continually being found out, which necessitates new means of communication. For Mount Desert direct, the favorite route from Boston is by rail to Rockland, and thence by steamer to Southwest and Bar Harbors: though such as have an unconquerable dread of the sea can proceed by rail to Bangor, and reach the island by the stage route. But thus they miss one great charm, namely, the ocean views of Mount Desert, which, to be thoroughly enjoyed, must be seen from every point of approach.

The outside route, by steamer from Portland, described in the Preface with others, has its advantages, as many prefer the long water route. Those who do not care to follow any of the routes described, may find their way to Mount Desert in accordance with the method indicated in the next chapter, the most independent, of course, though comparatively expensive.

Such as have a proper regard for health and comfort, will feel desirous of knowing how they are going to fare with respect to hotels. On this point, the advertiser's department of the Hand-book will give the particulars. It is only necessary to say, that the rough accomodations of former years have passed away ; and that the hotels, already very numerous, are managed with reference to the wants of the rapidly increasing throng which now annually finds its way to this wonderful Island.

There is much life and gaiety in the season at Mount Desert, and the visitor will find the same varied society usually seen at watering places ; the bad element excepted. There is much sociability amongst the people at the hotels, and less regard is paid to the strict conventionalities that prevail at many summer resorts. The foggy days may come, but the time need by no means be lost, as amusements are easily devised for the hours when it may be necessary to keep housed ; yet a season at Mount Desert will convince all true lovers of romantic scenery that their great entertainment is to be found

everywhere spread out of doors, free of cost to every
comer. It is this class for whom the author caters;
and if they cannot rest satisfied during a summer vaca-
tion with what the following pages offer, they will do
well by staying away from the New England coast altogether.

# *MOUNT DESERT.*

## CHAPTER II.

DEPARTURE FROM THE ISLES OF SHOALS — AGAMENTICUS —
NIGHT — SUNRISE — BECALMED — THE VIEW OF MOUNT
DESERT — ASHORE — THE MOUNTAINS.

ANDERING along the coast, we found
ourselves, in course of time, at the Isles of
Shoals, where we took passage in a trim-
looking schooner for Mount Desert. We
sailed in the morning with a fresh southerly breeze.
It was not long before we had a fine view of Agamenticus, which rises to the height of several hundred feet,
sending out its greeting from afar.

At this point, Mr. Oldstyle, the chief Historian of
the party, and who is really to be held responsible for
the most of what is said in the previous chapter,
felt a slight attack of sea-sickness; yet his unfailing
enthusiasm, united with the potent virtues of a lemon,
kept him up, and he managed to relate many things
about Agamenticus in the days of yore, and, among
others, that this place was early designed to be a
sort of metropolitan city. In 1642 Edward Godfrey
was duly appointed the mayor, while the same authority provided for two fairs to be "held and kept" there

"every year, forever thereafter" upon the Festivals of SS. James' and Paul's. The fate of this embryo city reminds us of the fact that the best laid plans of mice and men oft "gang agley." Nevertheless, Agamenticus forms a noble land-mark.

The Skipper here gave the coast a wide berth, and laid his course due north-east, shortly running down the land, though not before we had gained a glimpse of the distant peak of Mount Washington. The wind held fresh until sunset, and by nightfall the schooner was off Penobscot Bay, when the light-house on Mount Desert Rock opened its bright eye.

Our progress during the night was slow, but when morning dawned we were not far from the isle of our dreams. I was aroused from my slumbers by Old Sol himself, who, like some rude linkboy thrusting his torch in one's face, rose from the sea and sent a broad beam in through the little cabin window into my berth, hitting me squarely in the eye. Thereupon I resolved to rise. But Mr. Oldstyle, fully determined to have the first glimpse of the land, was ahead of me; and while I was pulling on my boots, disappeared up the companion-way in his smart, swallow-tailed coat, with a long spy-glass under his arm. Aureole, a young gentleman of our party, who, under the influence of Neptune, was very quiet the day before, followed him, having now got his "sea-legs" on ; and before I could get on deck I heard him engaging in the following brief colloquy :

" What land 's that, Skipper?"

"Mount Desert, I reckon," was the reply, putting the accent on the last syllable of " Desert."

" How far off?"

" Six or eight miles, ma' be."

"When are we going to get there ?"

" Don't know."

Thereupon I thought it high time to inquire into the real state of affairs; and accordingly I hurried on deck, and found that there was a dead calm, the mainsail hanging perpendicularly from its gaff, our little craft appearing altogether

> "As idle as a painted ship
> Upon a painted ocean."

Yet it was a splendid morning; and, besides, there lay our enchanted isle, towering up out of the calm sea, veiled in a thin mist, and gilded all over with the golden glories of the rising sun.

In order to find a scene that will equal this, we must sail far away into the Pacific Sea. At a distance the island appears like a single mountain, of great height, green around its sides, and bare at the summit, which, on this occasion, gleamed upon us through the mist like a pinnacle of gold.

We sat long gazing upon this beautiful prospect, not even desiring to come nearer, lest the vision should be dispelled. Yet with the sun came a light breeze, and as it approached in the distance, rippling the surface of the still sea, the Skipper unlashed the helm, and stood ready to steer his craft into port. And when the breeze came, it barely swung out the schooner's boom, though at last we managed to get steerage-way, and sailed slowly, wing and wing, and with a sort of classic pomp, the gull wheeling and the porpoise diving, and both showing a sort of welcome by escorting us on our voyage.

In due time we entered the Harbor, went ashore, and found comfortable quarters.

After being duly refreshed, we turned to the *Gazetteer,* and found it stated that Mount Desert is an island lying off the coast of Maine, at a distance of one hundred and ten miles east of Portland, being connected with the main-land by a bridge. Mr. Oldstyle, after consulting his notes, said that it was seen by Champlain in 1605, who called it *Mons Desert.* It is anything but a desert. Champlain judged of its character by the mountain-peak, so prominent when viewed from a distance, and which Whittier calls the "Bald mountain's shrubless brow," and

"The gray and thunder-smitten pile
Which marks afar the Desert Isle."

This land is to be distinguished from Mount Desert Rock, which lies in the ocean, fifteen miles south of the island, affording just room enough for the light-house. Mount Desert *Rock* is alluded to by Whittier, and I give his description, because it is as good as a photograph. He writes:

"And Desert Rock, abrupt and bare,
    Lifts its gray turret in the air —
    Seen from afar, like some stronghold,
    Built by the ocean kings of old."

This island contains about one hundred square miles. It is fourteen miles long, and, on an average, about seven wide, its longer axis lying nearly north and south. On the east side a tongue of the sea extends seven miles into the land, and is called Somes' Sound. On either side of the entrance to this Sound is a small harbor, one being called the North-east, and the other the South-west Harbor. Bar Harbor, where the steamer has a landing, is on the north-east side of the island. Here one of the Porcupine Islands is joined to Mount Desert by a sandy bar. Other islands are scattered around on every hand, adding greatly to the effect of the scenery.

But the mountains are the great distinguishing feature of the island. They are situated in its southern part, and form thirteen distinct peaks, which descend by gradual slopes towards the west, and end at the east, in most cases, with abrupt precipices, four of which look down upon glittering lakes, while a fifth reflects its image in the briny waters of Somes' Sound.

The highest peak is that of Green Mountain, upon which the officers of the Coast Survey built their observatory, and which served as the chief point in their complicated series of triangulations. The height of

this mountain is computed at fifteen hundred and
thirty-five feet above the level of the sea. These
mountains are the bones of the earth, which, being
broken and upheaved, form some of our most striking
and beautiful scenery, giving us lovely valleys, wild
mountain passes and sparkling fresh-water lakes, within
the sound of the murmuring sea. This leads to a remark on one feature of Mount Desert, which combines
the characteristics of seashore and inland, Newport
and the Catskills. I say the Catskills, and not the
White Mountains, because the great grandeur, and
often the sublimity of the latter, will not allow of a
comparison. Yet here we have the same *style*, if
not the same degree, of beauty. The White-Moun-
tain Notch is here represented, not unworthily, by the
celebrated Notch which is situated between Dry and
Newport Mountain, on the road from Bar Harbor
to Otter Creek. Wandering alone in the stillness of
this wild and romantic retreat, one can scarcely realize that he is indeed so near the shore of the loud-
sounding sea. Mrs. Browning's description of her
imaginary island applies with equal fitness to this,
when she writes:

"An island full of hills and dells,
   All rumpled and uneven
With green recesses, sudden swells,
   And odorous valleys, driven
So deep and straight, that always there
   The wind is cradled to soft air."

But all these features of Mount Desert, with its lakes and ponds and cliffs and trout-brooks and picturesque shores, will be described in detail elsewhere: so let us not anticipate the feast with a few crumbs.

# A RAINY MORNING WITH THE JESUITS.

## CHAPTER III.

A STORM BREWING — CONSULTATION — A VOTE FOR HISTORY — BIARD — A FALSE ALARM.

HAVING gained a general acquaintance with the place, posted ourselves with regard to the routes, and the best way of "doing" the island, an easterly storm came on, which promised to keep us indoors for a couple of days. A storm on the shore of Mount Desert affords many a fine sight, yet we did not come to see what Æolus could do in tossing breakers. Nevertheless, we accepted the situation, and when we found the gale rising, and the great raindrops dashing against the windows, we laid aside our canes and extemporized alpenstocks, and assembled in the little parlor for mutual counsel and advice.

And what should we do? Various propositions were made, but nothing seemed to meet the views of our party, which had been increased by the addition of three or four very pleasant and companionable persons,

many of whom we always find here.   Finally it was
proposed to have a reading, and one suggested that it
should be historic.   The countenance of our antiquarian friend, Mr. Oldstyle, beamed with satisfaction at
this, yet his expression quickly changed when Aureole,
a youthful family connection, broke out, saying, "Yes,
exactly, let us have Mr. Pickwick's monograph on
the source of Hampstead Ponds."   But Mr. Oldstyle met this exhibition of unseemly levity with such
a severe frown, and looked so concerned for the dig-
nity of history, that, while a young lady giggled, the
rest of the company quite failed to see the point of
the joke.   Therefore our worthy friend improved the
occasion to remind us of the wish expressed before
leaving home, to read the account of the planting and
destruction of the French colony of Mount Desert, on
the ground, and amid the scenes where the events occurred.   We therefore decided to have a Morning with
the Jesuits.   Mr. Oldstyle accordingly produced a roll
of manuscript containing a translation of Father
Biard's Narrative, as given in the first volume of
the *Relations des Jesuites*, recently published at
Quebec, "a better knowledge of which," said Mr.
Oldstyle, as he looked up at us over his spectacles,
"would have saved many writers on this subject from
serious blunders."

It is a notable fact that this subject has often
been treated with perfect recklessness.   Bancroft
states in the earlier editions of his History that

the French Colony of St. Savior was established on the
" north bank of the Penobscot," while his last revision
puts it on the *east side* of the Isle of Mount Desert.

The *date* of this attempt at colonization by the French
has seldom been stated with any accuracy, while in regard to the period of time spent by the French on the
island few seem to have known anything at all. Some
observations to this effect were made, and attention was
called to the fact that the old inhabitants of the isle were
reckless on this point. Whereupon Aureole confidently
offered the opinion that history was "all bosh, any
way."

Mr. Oldstyle received this remark of his young re-
lative with silent indignation; yet, while proceeding to
unroll his manuscript, he took occasion to confess that
history, and especially American history, was often
pursued in a spirit productive of little real good, the
truth being too often held subservient to popular
tradition.

Mr. Oldstyle, though somewhat advanced in years,
evidently leaned toward the new school of history,
now springing up, which is devoted to the elucida-
tion of Truth, without any reference to its cost. He
did not, however, think it worth while to enter upon a
discussion of these points; and, accordingly, after
briefly stating the reasons which led the French colonists to establish themselves on the coast of Maine,
in 1613, he began as follows:

## Father Biard's Relation.

"We were detained five days at Port Royal, by adverse winds, when a favorable north-easter having arisen, we set out with the intention of sailing up Pentegoët [Penobscot] River, to a place called Kadesquit, which had been allotted for our new residence, and which possessed great advantages for this purpose. But God willed otherwise, for when we had reached the south-eastern coast of the Island of Menan, the weather changed, and the sea was covered with a fog so dense that we could not distinguish day from night. We were greatly alarmed, for this place is full of breakers and rocks, upon which, in the darkness, we feared our vessel might drift. The wind not permitting us to put out to sea, we remained in this position two days and two nights, veering sometimes to one side, sometimes to another, as God inspired us. Our tribulation led us to pray to God to deliver us from danger, and send us to some place where we might contribute to His glory. He heard us, in His mercy, for on the same evening we began to discover the stars, and in the morning the fog had cleared away. We then discovered that we were near the coast of Mount Desert, an island which the savages call Pemetic. The pilot steered towards the eastern shore, and landed us in a large and beautiful harbor. We returned thanks to God, elevating the Cross, and singing praises with the holy Sacrifice of the Mass. We named the place and harbor St. Savior."

This harbor, Mr. Oldstyle thought, was North-east
Harbor, though, in the absence of authorities, he
would not be too positive. He then continued:

"Now in this port of St. Savior a violent quarrel
arose between our sailors and crew and the other passengers. The cause of it was that the charter granted,
and the agreement made in France, was to the effect
that the said sailors should be bound to put into any
port in Acadia that we should designate, and should
remain there three months. The sailors maintained
that they had arrived in a port in Acadia, and that
the said term of three months ought to date from this
arrival. To this it was answered that this port was
not the one designated, which was Kadesquit, and
therefore that the time they were in St. Savior was
not to be taken into account. The pilot held obsti-
nately to a contrary opinion, maintaining that no vessel had ever landed at Kadesquit, and that he did not
wish to become a discoverer of new routes. There
was much argument for and against these views, dis-
cussions were being carried on incessantly, a bad omen
for the future.

"While this question was pending," says the Father,
"the Savages made a fire, in order that we might see
the smoke. This signal meant that they had observed
us, and wished to know if we needed them, which we
did. The pilot took the opportunity to tell them that
the Fathers from Port Royal were in his ship. The
Savages replied that they would be very glad to see one

whom they had known at Pentegoët two years before. This was Father Biard, who went immediately to see them, and inquired the route to Kadesquit, informing them that he intended to reside there. 'But,' said they, 'if you desire to remain there, why do you not remain instead with us, who have as good a place as Kadesquit is?' They then began to praise their settlement, assuring him that it was so healthy and so pleasant, that when the natives were sick anywhere else they were brought there and were cured. These eulogies did not greatly impress Father Biard, because he knew sufficiently well that the Savages, like other people, overrated, sometimes, their own possessions. Nevertheless, they understood how to induce him to remain, for they said: 'You must come, for our Sagamore Asticou is dangerously ill, and if you do not come, he will die without baptism, and will not go to heaven, and you will be the cause of it, for he wishes to be baptized.' The reason, so naturally given, made Father Biard hesitate, and they finally persuaded him to go, since he had but three leagues to travel, and there would be no greater loss of time than a single afternoon."

Here the reader paused to tell us that one edition of Biard says that this spot was separated from the island of Mount Desert, which, by the French, was supposed to include only the land lying east of Somes' Sound. He then continued:

"We embarked in their canoe with Sieur de la Motte, and Simon, the Interpreter, and we set out.

"When we arrived at Asticou's wigwam, we found him ill, but not dangerously so, for he was only suffering from rheumatism; and finding this, we decided to pay a visit to the place which the Indians had boasted was so much better than Kadesquit for the residence of Frenchmen. We found that the Savages had in reality reasonable grounds for their eulogies. We felt very well satisfied with it ourselves, and, having brought these tidings to the remainder of the crew, it was unanimously agreed that we should remain there, and not seek further, seeing that God himself seemed to intend it, by the train of happy accidents that had occurred, and by the miraculous cure of a child, which I shall relate elsewhere.

"This place is a beautiful hill, sloping gently from the sea-shore, and supplied with water by a spring on each side. The ground comprises from twenty-five to thirty acres, covered with grass, which, in some places, reaches the height of a man. It fronts the south and east, towards Pentegoët Bay, into which are discharged the waters of several pretty streams, abounding in fish. The soil is rich and fertile. The port and harbor are the finest possible, in a position commanding the entire coast; the harbor especially is smooth as a pond, being shut in by the large island of Mount Desert, besides being surrounded by certain small islands which break the force of the winds and waves, and fortify the entrance. It is large enough to hold any fleet, and is navigable for the largest ships up to a cable's length from the shore. It is in latitude forty-four and one-half degrees north, a position more northerly than that of Bordeaux."

Mr. Oldstyle here also gave as his opinion that the place finally fixed upon as the site for their new habitation was located on the western side of Somes' Sound, on the farm of Mr. Fernald. The reader then went on:

"When we had landed in this place, and planted the Cross, we began to work, and with the work began our disputes, the omen and origin of our misfortunes. The cause of these disputes was that our Captain, La Saussaye, wished to attend to agriculture, and our other leaders besought him not to occupy the workmen in that manner, and so delay the erection of dwellings and fortifications.[1] He would not comply with their request, and from these disputes arose others, which lasted until the English obliged us to make peace in the manner I am about to relate."

Mr. Oldstyle omitted Biard's statement of the position of the English in America, in which he declares that the distance intervening between their colony and those of the French rendered all quarreling needless. Continuing:

"The English colonists in Virginia are in the habit of coming every year to the islands of Pencoit, twen-

(1) Here Father Biard leaves it undecided whether any fortifications were put up; but Charlevoix says that they "hastily threw up a slight entrenchment."

ty-five leagues from St. Savior, in order to provide
food [fish] for the winter. While on their way, as
usual, in the summer of the year 1613, they were overtaken out at sea by fogs and mists, which in this region
often overspread both land and sea, in summer.
These lasted some days, during which the tide drifted
them gradually farther than they intended. They
were about eighty leagues farther in New France than
they supposed, but they did not recognize the place."

Here our excellent friend, who never hesitated to
call a spade a spade, explained to us that this was the
ship of Samuel Argall, ostensibly a trader, but practically a pirate, like a large number of men of his
class, who, in those early times, roved the seas. He
had sailed the previous May for the Isles of Shoals,
to catch codfish, in a vessel carrying fourteen guns and
sixty men, and now he had lost his reckoning in the
fog, and improved the occasion to murder and plunder
the French. In his letter to Nicholas Hawes, said Mr.
Oldstyle, sarcastically, he speaks of his *fishing* voyage,
in which he beseeches "God of his mercy to bless us."
Aureole put in the remark, that " He was doubtless as
respectable a man as a good many others never found
out;" which remark, though felt, was ignored, as
Mr. Oldstyle was somewhat averse to the encourage-
ment of such unsettling opinions among the young.
Failing in this, the festive Aureole, who had been
sitting astride his chair, with his chin resting upon
the top bar, looking out of the window, now fancied

he saw a ship running into the harbor, through the driving rain and fog. He consequently interrupted the reading by calling the company to view this unexpected visitor, while Mr. Oldstyle laid aside his spectacles, and aimed mine host's spy-glass toward the point indicated by Aureole. But nothing could be seen, while Aureole himself suggested that it was the Flying Dutchman. Mr. Oldstyle, however, suspected that it was simply a ruse to break up the reading, which Aureole viewed as a sort of bore. Nevertheless, we all took our seats again, except Aureole, who went to look into the condition of his fishing-tackle, while Mr. Oldstyle benignantly put on his spectacles to resume the story. But the remainder must be reserved for the next chapter.

# A RAINY MORNING WITH THE JESUITS.

[CONTINUED.]

## CHAPTER IV.

ARGALL APPEARS — THE FIGHT — THE SURRENDER — DEATH
OF DU THET — THE FATE OF THE FRENCH — ARGALL'S
DEPARTURE AND RETURN — BIARD.

ILENCE once more prevailed in our little circle, though the storm continued without, and as we glanced across South-west Harbor, we saw that

"Thro' scudding drifts the rainy Hyades
Vext the dim sea."

Accordingly Mr. Oldstyle resumed the story, as follows :

"Some Savages observed their vessel and went to meet them, supposing them to be Frenchmen in search of them. The English understood nothing of what the Savages said, but conjectured from their signs that there was a vessel near, and that this vessel was French. They understood the word 'Normans,' which the Savages called us, and in the polite gestures of the natives, they recognized the French ceremonies of courtesy. Then the English, who were in need of provisions, and of every thing else, ragged, half naked, and in search of plunder, inquired carefully how large our vessel was, how many canoes we had, how many men, etc., and having received a satisfactory answer, uttered cries of joy, demonstrating that they had found what they wanted, and that they intended to attack us. The Savages did not interpret it so, however, for they supposed the English to be our friends, who desired earnestly so see us. Accordingly one of them guided the English to our vessel. As soon as the English saw us they began to prepare for combat, and their guide then saw that he had made a mistake, and began to weep and curse those who had · deceived him. Many times afterwards he wept and implored pardon for his error of us, and of the other Savages, because they wished to avenge our misfortunes on him, believing that he had acted through malice.

"On seeing this vessel approach us, we knew not whether we were to see friends or enemies, Frenchmen or foreigners. The pilot therefore went forward in a sloop to reconnoitre, while the rest were arming themselves. La Saussaye remained ashore, and with him the greater number of the men. Lieutenant La Motte, Ensign Ronfere, Sergeant Joubert, and the rest went on board the ship.

"The English vessel moved quickly as an arrow, having the wind astern. It was hung at the waist with red,

the arms of England floated over it, and three trum
pets and two drums were ready to sound. Our pilot,
who had gone forward to reconnoitre, did not return
to the ship, fearing, as he said, to fall into their hands,
to avoid which, he rowed himself around an island.
Thus the ship did not contain one-half its crew, and
was defended only by ten men, of whom but one, Captain Flory, had had any experience in naval con-
tests. Although not wanting in prudence or courage,
the Captain had not time to prepare for a conflict, nor
had his crew; there was not even time to weigh anchor, so as to disengage the ship, which is the first
step to be taken in sea fights. It would, however,
have been of little use to weigh the anchor, since the
sails were fastened; for, being summer, they had arranged them as an awning to shade the decks. This
mishap, however, had a good result, for our men being
sheltered during the combat, and the English unable
to take aim at them, fewer of them were killed or
wounded.

"As soon as they approached, our sailors hailed
them, but the English replied only by cries of men-
ace, and by discharges of musketry and cannon. They
had fourteen pieces of artillery and sixty artillerymen,
who ranged themselves along the side of their vessel,
firing rapidly, without taking aim. The first discharge
was terrible; the whole ship was shrouded in fire and
smoke. On our side the guns remained silent. Captain Flory cried out, 'Put the cannon in position,' but

the gunner was absent.  Father Gilbert du Thet, who had never been guilty of cowardice in his life, hearing the Captain's order, and seeing that no one obeyed, took the match and fired the cannon as loudly as the enemy's.  The misfortune was that he did not aim carefully; had he done so, probably something more useful than noise would have occurred.

"The English, after their first attack, prepared to board our vessel.  Captain Flory cut the cable, and thus arrested for a time the progress of the enemy.  They then prepared to fire another volley, and in this du Thet was wounded by a musket, and fell across the helm.  Captain Flory and three other men were also wounded, and they cried out that they surrendered.  The English, on hearing this cry, went into their boat to board our vessel, our men imprudently rushed into theirs in order to put off to shore before the arrival of the victors.  The conquerors cried out to them to return, as otherwise they would fire on them, and two of our men, in their terror, threw themselves into the water and were drowned, either because they were wounded or, more probably, were shot while in the water.  They were both promising young men, one named Le Moine, from Dieppe, and the other named Nenen, from Beauvais.  Their bodies were found nine days afterwards, and carefully interred.  Such was the history of the capture of our vessel."

Here the Honorary Member inquired if Mr. Bancroft did not say in his notice of the event that the

English bombarded the French fort. Mr. Oldstyle re-plied that he *did*, but that his statement lacked *autho*-*ity;* for himself, he would not take anything without "authority."

"Just so," said the Honorary Member ; while the Reader went on to recite, not wholly without indigna-tion, the story of Argall's perfidy :

"The victorious Englishmen made a landing in the place where we had begun to erect our tents and dwellings, and searched our Captain to find his com-mission, saying that the land was theirs, but that if we would show that we had acted in good faith, and under the authority of our Prince, they would not drive us away, since they did not wish to imperil the amicable relations between our two Sovereigns. The trouble was that they did not find La Saussaye, but they seized his desk, searched it carefully, and having found our commissions and royal letters, seized them, then putting everything in its place, they closed and locked the desk. On the next day, when he saw La Saussaye, the English Captain welcomed him politely, and then asked to see his commission. La Saussaye replied that his papers were in his desk, which was accordingly brought to him, and he found that it was locked and in perfect order, but that the papers were missing. The English captain immediately changed his tone and manner, saying, 'Then, sir, you are im-posing on us. You give us to understand that you hold a commission from your King, and yet you can

produce no evidence of if.   You are all rogues and
pirates, and deserve death.'   He then granted permis-
sion to his soldiers to plunder us, in which work they
spent the entire afternoon.   We witnessed the destruction of our property from the shore, the Englishmen
having fastened our vessels to theirs, for we had two,
our ship and a boat newly constructed and equipped.
We were thus reduced to a miserable condition, and
this was not all.   Next day they landed and robbed
us of all we still possessed, destroying also our clothing and other things.   At one time they committed
some personal violence on two of our people, which
so enraged them that they fled into the woods, like
poor crazed creatures, half naked, and without any
food, not knowing what was to become of them."

We now come, said Mr. Oldstyle, to learn the
fate of the brave ecclesiastic, who, while professional
soldiers fled, had the courage to stand by the guns:

"To return to the Jesuits:   I have told you that
Father du Thet was wounded by a musket-shot during the fight.   The English, on entering our ship,
placed him under the care of their surgeon, along with
the other wounded men.   This surgeon was a Catho-
lic, and a very charitable man, and he treated us with
great kindness.   Father Biard, knowing that Father
du Thet was wounded, asked the Captain to allow him
to be carried ashore, so that he had an opportunity to
receive the last Sacraments, and to praise the just and
merciful God, in company with his brethren.   He

died with much resignation, calmness, and devotion, twenty-four hours after he was wounded. Thus his prayers were granted, for, on our departure from Honfleur, he had raised his hands and eyes toward heaven, praying that he might return no more to France, but that he might die laboring for the salvation of souls, and especially of the Savages. He was buried the same day at the foot of a large cross which we had erected on our arrival.

"It was not till then that the English recognized the Jesuits to be priests. Father Biard and Father Ennemond Masse went to the ship to speak to the English captain, and explained frankly to him that they were Jesuits, who had travelled into these regions to convert the Savages. Then they implored him, by the blood of Him whom they both acknowledged as their Redeemer, and by the mercy they hoped for, that he would have pity on the poor Frenchmen, whom God had placed in his power, that he would liberate them, and permit them to return to France. The Captain heard them quietly, and answered them respectfully. 'But,' said he, 'I wonder that you Jesuits, who are generally supposed to be conscientious and religious men, should be here in company with robbers and pirates, people without law or religion.'

"Father Biard replied to him, proving that all the crew were good men, and approved by his Most Christian Majesty, and refuted so positively the objections of the English captain, that the latter was obliged to pretend to be convinced. 'Certainly,' said he, 'it was very wrong to lose your letters patent. However, I shall talk with your captain about sending you home.' And from that time, he made the two Fathers share his table, showing them much kindness and respect. But one thing annoyed him greatly, the escape of the pilot and sailors, of whom he could hear nothing. The pilot was a native of Rouen, named Le Bailleur; he had gone away to reconnoitre, as I have already mentioned, and being unable to return to the ship in time, he stayed apart in his sloop, and when night fell, took with him the other sailors, and placed himself in security from the power of the English. At night he came to advise with us as to what he had better do. He did this to oblige the Jesuits, for he came to Father Biard, and taking his hand, begged him not to distrust him, assuring him that he would be faithful to him and the other Fathers. As he seemed to speak sincerely, Father Biard thanked him affectionately, and promised to remember his kindness. The Father also said that he would not think of himself until the others had set out, that then he would seek counsel of God; and he warned the pilot not to fall into the hands of the English, because the captain was very anxious to catch him. The pilot profited by the warning, for in two or three days after, he retired behind some of the islands, to be in shelter, and to watch for what might happen. The English captain then resolved not to inflict any further injury on us, although he might have

desired to do so, as I conjectured by his previous conduct. He was a very able and artful man, but nevertheless a gentleman and a man of courage. His crew
were neither cruel or unkind to any of us."

The narrative was concluded as follows: "It is difficult to believe how much sorrow we experienced during this time, for we did not know what was to be our
fate. On the one hand, we expected either death or
slavery from the English; and on the other, to remain
in this country and live an entire year among the Savages, seemed to us a lingering and painful death. The
Savages, having heard of our disasters, came to us and
offered to do all in their power for us, promising to
feed us during the winter, and showing us great kindness. But we could not see any hope before us, and
we did not know how we could live in such a desert."

Mr. Oldstyle then told us, in brief, how a way was
opened for their disposition by this man whom the
Jesuit, who was soured against the French leaders,
curiously praises as a gentleman. La Saussaye, Father
Masse, and thirteen others were mercilessly cast off in
an open boat, instead of being put on board a French
vessel, as Bancroft says. This company, when joined
among the islands by the pilot and his boat, who fled
previous to the fight, made their way eastward by the
aid of oars, coasting chiefly along the shore until,
on the southern coast of Nova Scotia, they found
two trading-vessels, in which they secured a passage to
St. Malo. On the other hand, Father Biard and thir-

teen of the company were carried prisoners to Virginia, where Sir Thomas Dale, Governor of Virginia,
threatened them with the halter, so that Argall was
finally obliged to confess that he had stolen the com-
mission of La Saussaye from his desk at Mount Desert.
This theft was perpetrated to justify his own piracy,
for which he richly deserved to suffer the penalty of
the law, as the two nations were then at peace, and no
excuse whatever could be urged for this cruel deed.
Yet, said the narrator, they were not even satisfied
with the wrong and mischief that they had actually
done, and Argall soon fitted out his own ship and the
captured vessel of La Saussaye, together with a third
smaller vessel, for the purpose of destroying Port
Royal.   In this expedition they were accompanied by
Father Biard, who, according to certain English and
French writers, encouraged the attack " out of indi-
gestible malice " (Purchas, Vol. iv. 1808,) which he had
conceived against his old enemy, Biencourt, then in
charge at that place.   Biard himself gives the contrary impression, yet he allows that both the French
and English looked upon him as a traitor ; and, while
the English desired to hang him, one of the French
ended a parley with him at Port Royal by saying,
" Begone, or I will split your head with this hatchet."
Mr. Oldstyle thought that the Jesuit's character
needed looking into ; yet he went on to tell us how
Argall sailed the second time for St. Savior, expecting to find that another ship had arrived from France,

being still bent on plunder.　But he met no one except peaceful Indians.　Landing at this beautiful place, the English destroyed everything that remained.　Says Father Biard, "They burnt our fortifications and pulled down our crosses, and put up one as a sign that they were taking possession of the land as Lords. This cross had the name of the King of Great Britain engraved upon it."

Argall continued here some time, long enough indeed for one of his men to attempt a conspiracy against him, and thus these thieves fell out among themselves.　Yet the plan failed, and Father Biard writes that "they also hanged one of their men for a conspiracy in the same place where eight days before they had taken down the first of our crosses."

This ended Mr. Oldstyle's story, for which we all felt greatly obliged, the feeling of the party culminating in a vote of thanks.

The Colony of St. Savior therefore perished.　For this high-handed outrage the French, owing to the disturbed condition of European politics, were unable to obtain proper indemnification.　Madame de Guercheville only succeeded in recovering La Saussaye's ship.

As it may be interesting to the reader to learn the fate of Father Biard, we may relate here that Argall's fleet, on its return to Virginia from the destruction of Port Royal, was overtaken by a gale, in which one vessel was lost, while that in which the Jesuit sailed

was driven to the Azores.   The Commander, Lieutenant Turnel, afterwards decided to sail to Pembroke,
in Wales, where Father Biard was set ashore, being
well received by the Protestant Ecclesiastics.   From
thence he went to France, where, as a theological
Professor, he perhaps found more quiet employment
for a time, though he ended his days as a chaplain in
the army.

# SOMES' SOUND.

## CHAPTER V.

SUMMER tourists who enter Mount Desert by the way of South-west Harbor are liable to receive very unfavorable impressions of this beautiful island. While approaching the shore, the most charming views are obtained, but after the first salutation their majesties the mountains become shy, and when the steamer reaches the pier they are wholly lost to sight.

The visitor, however, must not be discouraged, for the reason that the mountains will soon re-appear. In fact, he will discover that South-West Harbor is not inferior to any other part of the Island, having advantages differing from those of Bar-Harbor, and which are peculiarly its own. The steamboat landing is at Clark's Point, upon which the Island House stands. This Point also shelters the harbor, which is well adapted for safe sailing. A large portion of the chief attractions are within easy reach, and the place soon grows upon the visitor who can easily fill up all the time allotted to his sojourn on the island. One of the loveliest places thus accessible is " Somes' Sound," a body of water, six or seven miles long, formed by an arm of the sea, which nearly divides the island in the middle. Admirable views of the sound may be enjoyed by a walk of five or ten minutes from the hotels to the east side of Clark's Point, where is found a rocky shore well suited to summer idling. Yet the best way to explore this part of the island is to take a boat and sail leisurely up to Somesville. It is the custom to start from South-west Harbor, and, rounding Clark's Point, to steer for Fernald's Point. The scenery thus appears to the best advantage. As we proceed, the sound, which is about two miles wide at the entrance, assumes the character of a noble river, fenced in by rugged mountains and fair green hills, the margin being diversified by points and coves. From a distance, looking up the sound, the view resembles that of the Delaware Water Gap, while on a nearer approach it forcibly brings to mind the Hudson at the Highlands. But here, however, there are no unsightly works of man to mar the prospect. An occasional cottage may be seen nestling among the hills, and the fishing-smack is found at anchor, the crew busily engaged in setting their nets, but otherwise nature appears in all her untamed wildness.

The entrance to the sound is shut in by islands, so that we do not realize our nearness to the sea; yet here, under the shadow of the hills, where we are

often reminded of Lake George, the fisher-boy hauls up
the portly cod and the haddock, while anon the whole
surface ripples with schools of herring and menhaden.

The sound cuts through the centre of the mountain-
range at right angles between Dog Mountain and
Mount Mansell, which name we gave to the elevation
on the eastern side, partly because it has heretofore
had no recognized name, but more especially for the
reason that at an early period the whole island was so
called by the English, in honor of Sir Robert Mansell.
This mountain is of no considerable height, yet it lends
great beauty to the prospect, its summit being more
or less bare. Dog Mountain, however, attains a fine
elevation, and reflects its perpendicular face in the
deep waters that sparkle around its feet. Through
the splendid gateway formed by these two mountains,
we pass into the broader waters beyond, and gain a
glimpse of the pastoral scenery which is found around
Somesville.

Within the protecting reaches of Somes' Sound, the
French decided to establish their new home. We
have already seen that the precise spot was at what is
now known as Fernald's Point. Towards this place
we laid our course with no little interest the first time
we were out boating, after the recital of Father
Biard's Narrative when storm-bound at the inn. It
was a charming day, and nearly the entire mountain-
range could be clearly distinguished, though the eastern sections were the most prominent, Green Moun-

tain lifting itself above all the rest, crowned by the little public house which marks its top. A pleasant breeze soon carried us on to Fernald's Point, a beautiful grassy piece of land which sweeps gently up from the shore, precisely as Father Biard describes it, terminating in a small but finely formed ridge of naked rock. Landing here, we walked over the ground, which includes very nearly the precise number of acres indicated by the Relation, and which are characterized by a rich and fertile soil. Here we looked down upon the harbor, " smooth as a pond," with the bold water navigable for the largest ships, " up to within a cable's length of the shore," and the entrance strongly fortified against wind and weather by rockbound yet sunny isles.

The account says that the place where the French settled, was " shut in by the large island of Mount Desert," a statement that appears to have misled some persons. The explanation was briefly given in a previous chapter, where the reader was informed that the French supposed the land on the west side of the sound to be wholly separated from that on the east, which, on account of the barren aspect of the mountains, they called Mount Desert. And now here lay before us the same old mountains of which the priest wrote. Mr. Oldstyle was charmed with the exactness of the description, which he rightly declared to be photographic, and incapable of application to any other spot on the coast of Maine.

While at the farm-house, we inquired if there were any springs of water on the Point, as Biard says that it " was supplied with water by a spring on each side." The query was promptly answered by Mr. Fernald, who led us to a spring on the east side, and one also on the west. That on the east side ran into the sound. Its outlet has been greatly disturbed by the wearing away of the shore, yet we found the water still running. That on the west side of the Point overflows into a little cove, boiling up out of the sand with considerable force. At high tide the salt water flows into it, yet when the tide recedes the spring is found as pure and fresh as before. This spring was running here when the ancestors of the Fernalds first settled on the land, and is beyond question the identical spring at which the Jesuit Fathers quenched their thirst in the summer of 1613. The water is cold and inexhaustible, fishing-fleets often coming here in dry season, when the wells fail, to fill their tanks and casks.

Of French relics there are none. The shell-heaps seen near the shore must be referred to the Indians, who evidently dwelt upon this sightly place. The graves of the French killed in the fight with Argall have never been discovered. Father Vetromile, in his work on the Abenakis Indians, indeed gives a picture purporting to represent the grave of du Thet, yet the sketch is a pure fancy, designed perhaps to impress the imagination of the faithful. At an early period

every vestige of the French completely passed away.
Back of Flying Mountain, and directly under Eagle
Cliff, in Dog Mountain, we were shown trenches, recently opened in connection with holes in the ground,
having the appearance of ancient cellars.   Our friend
Aureole, who went with us, made light of these
" cellars," while Mr. Oldstyle demonstrated that they
were formed, like many others which he afterward
showed in the woods, by the upturning of large trees.
The parties who opened these trenches gave us the
impression that they were laboring in the interests of
history, yet our own view is that they were influenced
by the mania for money-digging, of which something
is to be said by and by.   They evidently hoped to find
treasure buried by the French.

We left the place and returned to the Point, which
ought to be known as St. Savior, since the French
evidently transferred the name given to their first
landing-place to this ; and, after drinking once more
from the sparkling water of Father Biard's Spring, we
embarked and sailed past Flying Mountain, landing
upon the shore of the cove, not far from our friend's
"cellars."   Here a wrecked fishing-smack lay, quietly
going to pieces.   The place is one of very great
beauty, being hemmed in on the west by Eagle Cliff,
which rises to a height of eight or nine hundred feet.

Near this cliff is another, in the face of the same
mountain.   It looks down upon the deep water of
the sound, which is navigable for large vessels up to

its very base. It is altogether the most wonderful
cliff on the island, the granite faces, nearly a thousand feet high, being inaccessible to mortals. We
brought our boat under this dreadful precipice, where
we could look up squarely into the crags. The view is
sublime, but the position was one in which we did not
care to linger, as in many places detached rocks of
immense size seemed on the point of falling down.
At the foot of the precipice lay vast quantities of
*debris*, and we therefore gave the cliff a wide berth,
sailing past to a point which made out into the
sound. Here we landed, and discovered a place
where it was possible to ascend the mountain. The
course taken was well nigh perpendicular, and I was
left to climb alone from rock to rock, hauling myself
up by the stunted trees and shrubs, no one else caring
to undergo the labor.

Finally I reached the top, and walked along the
escarpment until I came to the edge of the perpendicular cliff. Here, looking down, the scene was most
impressive. The boat, with her white sail, now
seemed scarcely larger than a gull, while our party,
who had climbed up a short distance from the water
and perched themselves upon a jutting rock to await
the result of my adventure, were now reduced to
pigmies. I shouted aloud to Amarinta, but could not
make myself understood. I waved my hat, but was
not observed. I at last found that I must take a
position on the highest peak, where my figure would

stand out sharply defined against the sky. Here I was soon seen, and to my signal Amarinta's dainty pocket-handkerchief fluttered a reply. Then in response to my loud halloo, came a small voice. The cambric waved again, and I caught two syllables that floated slowly up from the depths below,—*Take care!* It was the small voice which belonged to the anxious proprietor of the pocket-handkerchief. As for Oldstyle, he viewed me through his glass with as much unconcern as though I had been an eagle or a crow; while Aureole lay prone upon the rock in utter idleness, thus saving the polish of his patent-leather boots.

All along the edge of the cliff the bare granite is full of horrid seams and rifts, while huge sections seem ready at any minute to plunge downward into the sound below. A hint from a handful of gunpowder would dislodge millions of tons. Here I was most forcibly reminded of Shakspeare's description of Dover Cliffs in King Lear, which applies to these, with the exception of the samphire-gatherer :

> " Come on, Sir; here's the place:—stand still.—How fearful
> And dizzy 'tis to cast one's eyes so low!
> The crows, and choughs, that wing the midway air,
> Show scarce so gross as beetles: half way down
> Hangs one that gathers samphire; dreadful trade!
> Methinks, he seems no bigger than his head:
> The fishermen, that walk upon the beach,
> Appear like mice; and yon, tall, anchoring bark,
> Diminish'd to her cock; her cock, a buoy
> Almost too small for sight: the murmuring surge
> That on the unnumber'd idle pebbles chafes,
> Cannot be heard so high."

Virgil says that the descent to Avernus is easy, yet
the descent of this Cliff is twice as hard as the ascent,
and requires double the time. It is finally accomplished, however, and after various slips and slides I
reached the rock where our boat was moored, when
we sailed out from under these frowning heights,
which gradually sink towards the north, forming a
valley, and then rise again pushing out into the sound.
This valley, which terminates on the sound, is ele-
vated only about forty or fifty feet above the water.
The bank is of shelving granite, down which pours a
small stream known as Man-of-War Brook, so called,
tradition tells us, from the fact that in the last war
with England the King's cruisers sailing along the
coast were accustomed to put in here to fill their
tanks. It certainly must have proved a convenient
place for this purpose. As we sat in the boat, rocking
gently upon the salt waves, our cups received the cool
sparkling water of the brook—a child of the uplands
—which even at this dry season was pouring down a
bountiful supply. It was here very pleasing to notice
the confidence of a pretty linnet, who alighted to share
with us the benefit of the brook, perching herself on
the point of a rock under the spray, and performing
her ablutions with all the nice airs of a high-bred city
bird.

On one side of the brook was a landing, and a
couple of wild, amphibious looking boys were pushing
out in a weather-beaten boat with an old black sail to

go after haddock. Their trade had early put its seal upon them. O flesh, how fishified! Two little girls, with bare heads and feet, sat on the bank staring at us with beautiful dark brown eyes. Their features were good, but when we spoke to them it was mournful to hear the elder, about ten years old, answer in a hoarse voice, which clearly implied much physical neglect. The sun was broiling hot, and we asked if she had no bonnet, being told in reply that she had one last summer. She had no shoes, and last winter she froze her feet. Their parents lived in a log-house up in the valley. Having heard that there were money-diggers in the neighborhood, we inquired for the place where they were at work. The girls pointed up the valley and led the way. A short walk brought us to a wild and romantic spot where the ground had been partially cleared, and where granite cliffs, sprinkled with shaggy fir and spruce, rose up on the north side to a height of three or four hundred feet. In the middle of the cleared ground was an excavation large enough for the cellar of a good-sized house. The excavation extended down to the solid rock, which everywhere underlies the drift, and a couple of strange-looking men were hard at work with long-handled spades throwing out the earth. These were the money-diggers, whose faith was soon to be rewarded with untold treasures of silver and gold.

The history of money-digging in Maine is somewhat curious. There has scarcely ever been a time when the subject did not attract attention. Kendall, in his Travels, gives an account of a great sensation created in connection with the subject in the beginning of the present century, at Norridgewock, where a man and his two sons gave out that they had found immense treasures, and, on the strength of the representation, swindled the community out of a large amount of property. At that time a person was going about in the interior lecturing on the subject of hidden treasure, and exciting the imagination of the people.

From time to time money has actually been found. Not long since a pot of gold and a signet-ring were discovered on Richmond Island, near Portland, by a farmer, Mr. Hanscom, when ploughing. Four hundred dollars in French crowns were found in a field near Frenchman's Bay. Near Castine a large collection of old coins was found by Captain Stephen Grindle in the year 1840–1. The place pointed out is on the bank of the Bagaduce, six miles from the site of the fort. At this point, perhaps, was the old road to Mount Desert.

About the close of November, 1840, Captain Grindle was engaged with his son, hauling wood down to the shore, when the latter picked up a piece of money near a partially buried rock, lying about seventy-five feet from the shore, and in the old line of a beaten track that had existed for time out of mind. Tradition likewise says that one of the Indian routes from the

peninsula of Castine to Mount Desert and Frenchman's Bay was up the Bagaduce, and thence across to
Blue-Hill Bay.

The coin found was a French piece. This prize
led them to commence digging in the ground, which
they continued doing until dark, the search being
rewarded by nearly twenty additional coins. During
the night the snow fell, and nothing more was done
until spring, when two coins were found embedded in
the top of the rock. An iron bar thrust into the
opening revealed the presence of a large quantity,
numbering nearly five hundred pieces of different
nations. Mr. Grindle's wife gleefully held her apron,
which was soon loaded by her husband and son, she
at the same time declaring that it was "the best lapful
she had ever carried."

These may have been lost or hidden by Baron
Castine, when, in 1688, he fled to the woods to escape
from Governor Andross. One of the silver coins was
recently shown me at Somesville by the person who
received it from the finder.

Still nearer this spot, on the east side of the sound,
opposite Fernald's Point, money has also been found.
At least such is the common belief, which is based on
good evidence. The reputed finder still lives (1868)
on the place, where, according to the testimony of a
man once in his employ, he discovered a pot of gold.
At all events his circumstances appear to have suddenly changed, when he rose from a condition of hard-

ship to one of comparative affluence and ease. That
gold may have been buried there is not at all unlikely.
When Argall attacked St. Savior, a part of the
French were scattered in the woods and among the
neighboring islands, and gold may have been buried
by them at the place in question and never recovered.

All these circumstances, taken together, lead the
somewhat credulous farmers and fishermen to imagine
that gold is everywhere buried on their lands. This
suspicion is strengthened by Spiritualists and Divining-
rod men, who go from place to place, practicing upon
the unsophisticated. We found one of the Spiritualists here in this valley. He was a man of somewhat
good features with gray beard and hair, and a wild
light in his eye. The diggers at first gave us the
impression that they were making a cellar, but gradually the owner of the ground, a red-faced man, half
farmer and half fisherman, unfolded the tremendous
secret. Mr. Oldstyle and the rest did not enjoy his
confidence, and it was reserved for my own ear to
enjoy the revelation in full.

Drawing me aside, he began by requesting my
opinion on the general subject of gold, and desired to
know if the rock was gold-bearing, and whether, in
case treasure was found, the United-States Government could take it away. I assured him that the
rocks of Mount Desert were not auriferous, and that
it was folly to look for treasure; moreover, that I
thought, so far as the Government might be concerned,

he would be welcome to all that he could find.  My
unbelief caused him to warm up, and to declare in a
low tone approaching a stage-whisper, "There's gold
here."    This did not produce the startling effect
anticipated, and therefore, with a sort of insanity blaz-
ing from his eyes, he went on to unfold his belief.
He had signified in the beginning that the object in
view was a cellar, because he did not know who I was.
I might have been a spy, or the agent of some party
about to make a midnight raid upon the diggings.
But now that he felt assured he was dealing with an
honest tourist, he had no objection to telling me that
they were in search of gold, and that in three days
they would reach it.    All the predictions made thus
far by the Spirits had been verified.   They had told
them that as he proceeded he would find the name of
one of the men originally engaged in depositing the
treasure, engraved on a plate.    The plate with the
name—JAMES LONG—had now been found, at least
such was his belief, though the man who discovered it
did not like to show it, but rather preferred to keep
them in the lively exercise of faith.    The treasure
buried was none other than the long-sought treasure
of the Pirate Kidd.    It lay under a black marble
slab, thirty feet square, and beautifully polished, resting on corner-stones, with a ring-bolt in the centre.
They were sure to have it in three days.

Having thus delivered himself, and finding that I
was not disposed to bid high for his claim, he cooled

off, and, instead of digging in the excavation with his
friends, very prudently went away into a corner of
his clearing and began to hoe potatoes. But the
others showed a more genuine faith, and continued
to ply their spades, at the same time expressing their
happy expectation. For himself, Graybeard did not
follow the example of the man who had just left me
for his hoe. *He* made no secret of it with *any* one.
He expected *gold.* He was at work for a good pay-
master, who would pay when the work was done.
I fervently hoped that it was so; but then, would his
work ever be *done?* The notion was scorned. There
could be no mistake. The treasure was already within their grasp. He had talked with Kidd, and knew
all about it; and so he plied his spade with fresh zeal.

This was the end of the controversy, and we prepared to leave. Whereupon one of the diggers came
out of the hole and inquired for " the axe," and began
to circle about a small tree under which Amarinta
sat, all the while in his gyrations approaching nearer
and nearer. Accordingly Amarinta became alarmed,
and rushed out of the charmed circle. Of this the man
took no notice; but finding his axe, instead of proceeding to slaughter, he quietly regained his hole in the
ground, where we heard him beating the dents out of
a shovel, preparatory to a fresh raid upon the inexhaustible treasures of Robert Kidd.

Thus we came off whole, notwithstanding the
proprietor told Aureole that he had twenty loaded

muskets standing just inside his door, an announce-
ment that made him feel nervous. As we turned and
left the diggers in the wild glen, Mr. Oldstyle tried to
calculate how much gold they might have actually
found if they had devoted the weeks spent upon this
huge excavation to honest tillage; while, when we
reached the boat, Aureole found his voice, and struck
up,

" My name was Captain Kidd, as I sailed, as I sailed."

The next place on the west side is the Crows' Nest,
the north spur of Dog Mountain, which descends
abruptly into bold water, covered with scraggy woods
from the summit down to the shore. Opposite, and
now near at hand, on the east side, is Mount Mansell,
which, with the Crows' Nest, forms the Narrows.
The view is singularly fine, and after sailing through,
the prospect widens, the sound being about three
miles from shore to shore. On the east side is seen
the little inlet called, like a larger bay on the west side
of the island, Seal Cove. Here they formerly caught
seal in abundance, but now a fish-house signifies that
the chief product is herring or menhaden. On the
west shore, a little way from the Crows' Nest, is a
granite slide called Denning's Walk. It covers a
large area, and dips to the water at a sharp angle,
being beautifully embossed with moss and lichen,
while here and there a small spruce struggles for life
in some narrow fissure of the rock. A long while

ago, on a dark winter night, a vessel was driven upon
the shelving rock and went to pieces, one of the crew
saving himself from freezing to death by walking on
the slide until daylight.

As we sail upward the land around us sinks nearly
to the level of the water, giving glimpses of the more
distant mountains, while the spire of Somesville, erelong, peeps out from among the trees. From the
Crows' Nest to this place is about three miles. We
enter the little harbor near the head of the sound by
passing through a narrow passage between an island
and the shore and land near a shipyard that has a
saw-mill attached. Everywhere from the upper part
of the sound we have beautiful views, Mount Mansell
sinking down into comparative obscurity, while Sargent's Mountain and Green Mountain loom up finely
beyond the intervening woods.

Towards the east a branch of the sound extends a
little higher up, and there vessels resort to load with
lumber ; while at Somesville it receives the fresh
water that flows down from the outlets of Long Lake,
on its way turning the ancient mill-wheels, which,
like river-gods at enforced service, laboriously grind
and saw.

Somes' Sound enables us to sail through the heart
of the best scenery on the island, to which it gives a
general introduction, thus preparing us to take up
other portions of this wonderful place in detail.
Wherever the boatman voyages, the eye is delighted

by new and ever-changing views, pleasant valleys— the home of the deer—inviting us ashore for a ramble, while the mountains pencil their features around us on the waves.

With a good breeze, a sail of a couple of hours will take visitors back to South-west Harbor, though whoever has the time will find it profitable to remain **at Somesville** for several days.

# AMONG THE MOUNTAINS.

## CHAPTER VI.

Western Mountain — Beech Mountain — Storm Cliff — Dog Mountain — Climbing — A Story — Flying Mountain — The French — Sargent's Mountain.

MOUNTAINS form one of the grandest features of this island; and Somes' Sound, by dividing them into two general groups, affords a convenient classification.

All the mountains on the west side are best reached from South-west Harbor, while those on the east, with the exception of Mount Mansell and Sargent's Mountain, should generally be ascended from Bar Harbor. On the west side are Western, Beech, Dog, and Flying Mountains, of which we are first to speak. These mountains may be distinguished from the others by a more verdant aspect, and a heavier growth of wood The name of Western Mountain indicates its position on the west shore of the island, overlooking Penobscot Bay. Seen from the water, it has a tolerably sharp peak, which, as we sail around the island, assumes somewhat the form of a sugar-loaf, apparently with a tendency to topple over towards the east. Yet this cone is very firmly fixed in its place, and will never cause alarm.

From South-west Harbor the mountain is very easily reached, as a carriage-road extends for a large portion of the way, changing to a wood-road on its side, which eventually fades out. This mountain has no great reputation, yet it is in every respect a beautiful height, affording a fine view of Penobscot Bay. Seal Cove Pond, a large and handsome sheet of water, lies along its eastern side, bathing its feet and reflecting its image at times as in a glass. From the pond, the sides of the mountain sweep upward like the sides of an amphitheatre, the wood-crowned ledges rising tier on tier.

Beech Mountain is far more popular than Western Mountain, from which it is separated by Long Lake. The same road that leads to the latter will conduct us to the former, if we are careful to turn in season to the right. The mountain road passes completely over between the two highest peaks, and descends northward to the village of Somesville. On the summit, and along the south side, it is extremely rough, and not adapted to public travel, yet with a strong wagon it is passable. This route is the one that would naturally be selected, and yet to ascend from Somesville is more pleasing. It involves eight or nine miles of additional travel, but whoever has the time to spare will not regret the labor. The road to Somesville is nearly seven miles long, and thence, turning to the left, it is two and a half miles to the first peak, called

the Nipple. The ascent is very gradual, and the hill
is round as a whale's back. It is covered with fields,
farms, and grass-lands, and on the latter were whole
seas of buttercups and daisies, waving in rare beauty
before the morning sun. We came this way ourselves, and as we ascended it was delightful to study
each new expanding scene. Reaching the base of the
first peak, we left our carriage and walked to the top,
where the prospect proved quite enchanting. Northward, the mountain descended gently to Somesville;
beyond were the Narrows, where the island keeps
tryst with the main, which here is fenced in by some
low but fine hills; eastward lay Denning's Lake, the
peaks of Dog Mountain, the Gold-Diggers' Glen,
Somes' Sound bordered by green woods and but-
ressed in the centre by Mansell, and beyond were the
heights of Goldsborough, smiling upon the encircling
bay : westward we marked the graceful summit of Blue
Hill, the distant reaches of Penobscot Bay gemmed
with fair isles and crowned by the Camden Heights;
while directly before us were the slopes of Western
Mountain, rising gracefully from the shadowy waters
of Long Lake, which slumbered in peace at our
feet.

Descending, we regained the road, and went on to
still higher ground, turning to the left among the fields,
and working our way on foot towards the eastern
summit, near which we looked down one of those
tremendous cliffs abounding in this island, and viewed

the waters of Denning's Lake.    Storm Cliff is of great height, and, like those of Dog Mountain, it drops perpendicularly to the water, the face being totally inaccessible.    It appears to the finest advantage, however, from the opposite side of the lake, which is skirted by the Somesville road, and the passer may thus get a glimpse of it through the trees.    But it is best to go down to the edge of the lake, where the cliff rises directly in front in all its majesty.    When lashed by the storms, which rave around these hills with the fury of fallen angels, the view is sublime. How do the misty battalions charge upon the living rock, and then break and fly!    There is certainly a soul in them; and even now the memory of a stormy day on that shore allures me down from sunny slopes and shady ridges to view once more their great conflicts.

But there is a third peak of Beech Mountain to climb, and when we leave the rough road and scale this granite cone, it becomes no trifling work.    Amarinta could not do it, and so was left for a little while to the companionship of a couple of kind, motherly-looking cows, and I scrambled up to the top.    From the summit of a rock all that was seen from the first peak now appeared in fresh beauty, with the additional prospect of the opening towards the south, which revealed South-west Harbor, the mouth of Somes' Sound, Bass Harbor, the eastern islands, and the boundless sea.

It would have been a pleasure to delay here for hours, but it was necessary to descend. Nor did I get back any too soon, for while I was gone an unruly steer joined the peaceful party left below, lashing his tail at the air so furiously, that Amarinta had taken possession of the reins, and was about to drive off and leave me to tramp home on foot. We returned to South-west Harbor, by the way of the rough mountain road, greatly delighted with the trip.

Dog Mountain is the local name of the eminence rising on the border of the sound. From one position towards the south it appears to be an immense mass of granite, nearly flat on the top, and with no comeliness to recommend it. On the Somesville road, near Denning's Lake, we get some idea of its altitude, and catch a glimpse of numerous steep, bare ledges; but it will not be appreciated until thoroughly climbed. The reader has already been introduced to one of its cliffs, and the Gold-Diggers' Glen, yet there is much remaining that will repay study.

The height of this, as well as of the other mountains, except Green Mountain and Newport, is not known, and we are only left to conjecture. Dog Mountain falls below Beech Mountain in altitude, yet, rising as it does directly from the water, not an inch is lost in the general effect by the interference of other objects. This, indeed, is an advantage possessed by all these sea-girt mountains, which, while lower than the Cats-kills, always equal and often exceed them in effect.

The ascent of Dog Mountain is easier than that of any of the higher peaks.  Three quarters of an hour from South-west Harbor, taking the right-hand road to Fernald's Point, will bring a good walker to the place where he begins the ascent, which is near the valley, terminating in the cove.  The route lies through sheep-walks and over bare ledges, and is occasionally obstructed by small spruces or pines. Keeping well to the right, the escarpment of the cliffs is reached, and the way is plain to the highest peaks.

Gaining the first elevation, we find that it terminates in a lofty precipice called Eagle Cliff, turning away from the sound and facing the beautiful valley formed by Flying Mountain, which now appears scarcely higher than a molehill.  I climbed it alone on the Fourth of July.  The sun was intensely hot, sufficiently so, indeed, to nearly boil one's brains How grateful was the cool breeze along this magnificent height, and how lovely the view both on the sound and at sea!

The last half a mile was a scramble over great disjointed rocks upheaved in the Titanic past, and here and there covered with dense thickets.  At last I reached the apex, marked by a rude cairn, to which every right-minded tourist is expected to contribute a stone.  On looking about, it is found that this mountain is the most barren of the western group, and that, instead of being flat-topped, it has a well-defined peak rising far above the first landing-place, which had the appearance of being the summit. The view towards the west is shut in, more or less, by Beach Mountain. Denning's Lake, which lies so near at the west, is invisible. The finest views are had up and down the sound. Here we are able to look into the neighboring valleys and ravines and inspect the physical peculiarities of this highland region, which is everywhere deeply scarred by the old geological agents. The development of the trap-rock is very marked. Intrusions, varying in width from three to thirty feet, may be traced along the axis of elevation. In one place I noticed that the face of the trap had been laid bare by a fault in the granite, exposing an immense wall forty or fifty feet high. These veins may undoubtedly be traced for miles, their extent indicating the vast destructive powers which nature has in store, powers that, if unchained, would soon cause all the elements to hiss and bubble in the fervent heat.

What studies in rock are here unfolded to the painter, as well as to the geologist! How gloriously crag is piled on crag, now laid firmly together with masonic skill, and now gaping with seams and rents, instantly threatening to fall!

With reluctance I rose from my hard couch under the shadow of the cairn, and, after casting a farewell glance into the Gold-Diggers' Glen, so replete with romantic beauty, I began my tramp downward. Reaching the brow of the precipice overlooking the cove, I paused again, enchanted by the beauty of the scene. It was now high noon, the breeze had died away, and a dead calm prevailed. The sound lay before me smooth as a sea of glass; nearer was the green cove, where the brick-red cows sought the shade of the rocks: while Flying Mountain rose up beyond like some fair green altar prepared for sacrifice. All sounds around me were hushed in this hour of noontide calm, and only the report of an occasional Liberty gun came booming across the waters of Penobscot Bay. I sat here long to gaze upon this scene of enchantment, and at the same time called to mind an incident about the cliff which was told me one day by a farmer as we walked in the cove below, considering the all-absorbing question of buried gold.

Looking up at these granite walls, I asked if it was possible to scale them. He replied that it was not, though he had been able to make his way up at the side. One of his sheep, it appears, had slipped part way down the cliff, and alighted upon a projecting ledge. The poor creature was unable to extricate herself from this perilous position, not having the power to get either up or down. Here upon this narrow pasture, where a sudden blast might whirl her off, and make mutton of her on the cruel rocks hundreds of feet below, she managed to browse for nearly a fortnight, subsisting upon moss and accidental moisture, while her piteous cries daily fell fainter and fainter in the farmer's ear. At last a man, moved

with pity, volunteered on Sunday afternoon to attempt
a rescue. Armed with a long pole, he tried to make
his way down to the ledge, and when last seen he was
lying upon his face, searching out a passage. A
minute afterwards those anxiously watching him suddenly found that he had disappeared. The discovery
filled them with consternation. Looking above they
could not see him retreating, and the conclusion was,
that he had fallen unobserved, and was dashed in
pieces. The alarm was raised, the neighbors assembled, and after a diligent but fruitless search, they
concluded to give it up. But before returning, they
raised a united shout, calling the man by name, if,
haply, he might still be alive. And the echo had
hardly died away when the man came out through
the bushes of the cove and stood unharmed before
them. Here was a miracle? Not quite; for, instead
of tumbling down the cliff, he became frightened and
crawled back through a crevice in the rock, afterwards
descending the opposite side of the mountain to visit
a neighbor, from whose house he was now returning
home. The people felt greatly relieved, though somewhat foolish; but the faint cry of the poor sheep still
floated down from her narrow prison. It was accordingly resolved to make a fresh attempt, and a rope
having been provided, a sailor was let down to the
ledge. After some effort, he brought up the famished
creature in his arms. As for the brave fellow himself,
he was drowned but a little while ago. On a cold

winter night his vessel was running for Squam Light
in a thick snow-storm, when she struck the beach,
bilged, and burned up.

So much for the story; and now 'here were the
cliffs before me, gray, steep, and perilous as ever.
And could I get down? *Hoc labor est.* I certainly
thought the difficulty had been overrated and began
to beat about in every possible place to find some way
to descend. But after cautiously trying a hundred
and fifty feet the difficulty grew more and more
apparent, and the way was at last barred by one of
those perpendicular walls of granite that yield to
no argument or persuasion. Discretion was here the
better part of valor, and accordingly I climbed back
to the summit again, where I caught the faint halloo
of a boating-party on the strand. They saw me
up among the crags, reduced in the distance to a
speck, and sent up their salutations. They acknowledged my own with a waving of hats; but Echo took
it up and sent it back with perfect distinctness from
the far-off sides of Mount Mansell. Just then a light
breeze swept down through the cove, kissed the white
sails of the little yacht, and bore her away.

Flying Mountain is a pigmy among the hills, yet
here the lover of the beautiful would build his cha-
teau. It was observed, as a matter of course, in our
trip up the sound, but it now requires more particular consideration. Its situation is unequalled. It

seems as if placed here to afford the best possible
out-look upon the lovliest scenery of the sound. The
approach is quite romantic. Soon after leaving the
turn of the road at the head of South-west Harbor,
the mountain lifts itself up to great advantage beyond
the fields, yet when we reach a given point near the
cove it affords a pleasing surprise, breaking into view
through the trees, with a part of Dog Mountain appearing on the left.

It is moreover a place that all can visit. Mr. Oldstyle was delighted because it was historic ground;
yet he confessed that its easy slopes suited his legs.
He would none of your tramps and forced marches
through tangled woods and dells. That would do for
poachers and boys. He often shook his head at our
folly. But now he felt that he had an object before
him. This was the beautiful hill of Father Biard, of
Masse, and of Brother Gilbert du Thet. So, planting his gold-mounted stick in the compact soil, he
nimbly trod the beaten path of the woolly sheep and
ascended to the summit, where he seated himself
upon a rock, and, slightly accommodating a quotation from Shakspeare, delivered himself as follows:

> "This *Mountain* hath a pleasant seat; the air
> Nimbly and sweetly recommends itself
> Unto our gentle senses."

Thereupon he laid aside his broad-brimmed hat, and
allowed the soft summer breeze to wander at will

among his locks. We left him to view at leisure the green fields below, where the French built their little fort, set up their tents, raised the Cross, sang the *Mass*, and chanted *Vexilla regis prodeunt;* to look down upon the calm waters of the sound, where Argall's ship came on "swift as an arrow," pouring in her broadside against the French; to see du Thet springing to the guns with the spirit of a hero, but quickly falling to welter in his own blood; to see the unequal fight, the speedy surrender, the pillage of the tents, the solemn funeral of the slain, and, finally, the departure of Argall, leaving the devastated camp wreathed in smoke. These things have now all passed away, yet to our antiquarian friend they are vivid realities. Gilbert du Thet's ashes rest somewhere beneath yonder greensward, the spring from which he drank still flows out from under the loins of this hill, the mountains upon which he gazed remain, the same ocean breaks upon the shore, and the same stars and sky look down from above. A single effort of the imagination re-creates the scene. So let us give Mr. Oldstyle a few minutes to himself, and we will scramble along the ridge of the mountain, which now assumes a wilder aspect, being broken up and seamed with trap, and sentinelled here and there with the half-burnt trunks of pine.

At the termination of the ridge the mountain descends abruptly to the sound, leaving no beach. It is therefore impracticable to pass around on the water side,

except with a boat. The view of the neighboring
mountains from this point is most lovely. It seems as
if one could almost throw a stone up among the crags
of Eagle Cliff opposite, while Thunder Cliff bears on
its front the characteristics of a palisade. Sweeping
away towards the middle of the sound is the north
spur of Dog Mountain, while Mount Mansell, in a
friendly mood, seems to advance from the east. Here
we have a fresh view of the jutting cliffs of the Gold-
Digger's Glen, and mark the seamed sides of the distant heights, which are written all over with records
of the Ancient of Days. Towards sunset the view
will perhaps appear to the best advantage, as at that
time the lengthening shadows bring out more clearly
the structure of the neighboring cliffs, while the red
granite bosses of Sargent and Green Mountain assume a softer glow. From this place we can look
away in any direction landward, and peep into pic-
tured alcoves and down shining vistas, or, turning from
the mountains, gaze across the sunlit islands upon the
purple sea. All is sweetness, beauty and repose.

I selected Somesville as the point of departure for
Sargent's Mountain on the east side of the sound.
The ascent can be accomplished by crossing the sound
from South-west Harbor, yet few persons, when at
Somesville, will be able to resist the temptation to
make a trip to this inviting height, which lifts itself
up in the distance before the door of the little home-

like hotel. The foot of the mountain may be reached either by boat or carriage. In the latter case it will be necessary to take the road to North-east Harbor. The route by water is pleasanter, as it affords charming glimpses down the sound. A brisk row of three-fourths of an hour brings us to a place called Seal Cove, like one of the inlets on the west shore of the island, where seals were formerly taken in abundance. Here we left the boat, struck across the fields, and found a wood road running along the base of the mountain. My guide evidently knew as little about the route as I did, yet I thought it well to have him along. Some men who were hoeing potatoes replied to my inquiries in a way that showed a slight degree of contempt for city folk. They "guessed," too, that I meant to stay on the mountain all night, thereby intending to reflect on the judgment exhibited in commencing the ascent in the middle of the afternoon. Unable to learn anything from these churls. who had lived here all their lives, we pursued the word road until it became reduced to a sort of squirrel-track, and then moved straight up the pathless side of the mountain. Thickets, dense foliage, and fallen trees everywhere obstructed the way, and a hard struggle was often required in order to open a passage. Occasionally the steep ledges intervened, from which glimpses were had of the expanding prospect, while it often appeared as if the summit lay within a few rods. Yet for a long, toilsome hour and a half, ledge rose on ledge. Finally the apex was reached and the reward gained. Every way the prospect exceeded my anticipations. From a distance the summit of the mountain appeared round and smooth, but when actually climbed it was found to be the most broken and rugged eminence on the island, and at the same time the most barren and desolate. The top occupies a large area full of rifts that, lower down, assume the character of chasms and ravines, among which everything except the sky is frequently lost to view. Mount Mansell, which lies between Sargent's Mountain and the sound, is scarcely seen from the northern part of the summit, the view being obstructed by a spur of Sargent that is separated from the main peak by a wild ravine with nearly perpendicular walls. Eastward, however, there is a fine view of Green Mountain brought out in bold relief by the declining sun.

Following the ridge of Sargent's Mountain southward about half a mile, a view of Eagle Lake is had, lying far down among the hills in the shade, and sparkling, at the evening hour, like a black diamond. A little farther south, in a cup-like depression of the ridge, is the Lake of the Clouds, a small body of water about an acre in extent, and which, according to fable has no bottom. Yet a line let down from a raft once gave a depth of sixteen feet. It is supplied chiefly by the winter snows. This lake lies in what resembles an ancient crater, though the rock is of granite and no signs of volcanic action are visible. Indeed, every

thing indicates the action of ice and frost. Agassiz,
when here, noted the resemblance of this mountain
to the Swiss hills that have been shaped by glacial
action. The summit is everywhere worn and rounded
by vast icefields five or six thousand feet thick, which
the great savan tells us crushed their way down from
the high regions of Katahdin to the sea. No less
stupendous a force could have accomplished such
results.

From this part of the mountain the view is open
towards the south, giving a view of Hadlock and Jordan's Ponds, North-east Harbor, and the neighboring
regions, with the broad Atlantic beyond.

As I left the margin of the Lake of the Clouds, the
sun threw his slanting beams against the rose-colored
granite wall that shuts it in on the south, when the
rocks began to mirror themselves in the water, flinging
down their warm tints upon the rushes and lily-pads
which were growing green among the delicately pen-
cilled images of the dwarfed spruce and pine.

The descent was accomplished by a different and
still more difficult route. A tolerably easy way could
have been found along by Jordan's Pond, yet my
destination was Somesville ; and, therefore, after
scrambling downward a short distance, in a southerly
direction, we took the range of prominent points on
Mount Mansell and prepared to move westward down
across the deep valley to the North-east Harbor road.
But here the wild beauty of the scene delayed me for

a little while, notwithstanding the night was coming on, and a long tramp was still to be accomplished. There, a thousand feet below, lay a long verdure-clad valley, sweeping down from the rifted summit and sides of Sargent's Mountain, into which, through rocky defiles, the setting sun threw long lances of light that only served to render the fast-gathering shade more impressive. But what proved equally beautiful was the music of the birds, which from the day I first stepped ashore at Mount Desert never ceased to prove a source of delight. And now the whole valley rang with song, and, as a dead calm prevailed, every note was caught up and echoed among the mountains, the effect being as singular as it was beautiful.

But I was soon admonished by my guide of the necessity of pushing on, and therefore I reluctantly sought the edge of the declivity and slid down from rock to rock among the trees, until I reached an open place near the centre of the valley, where I could look up at the crag which I had just left. Then, pushing into the dense woods, we beat our way through the under-brush, amidst the fast-gathering gloom, until, long after sunset, we joyfully emerged upon the road which passes under the perpendicular cliffs in the east side of Mount Mansell. The walk here in this notch is always fine, but at twilight it is unusually interesting.

A rapid walk of two miles northward brought us to the cove in Somes' Sound, where we had left the boat.

It was soon launched, and speeding on its way, impelled by two flashing oars. On this occasion I had an opportunity of witnessing the effect of a summer twilight on this beautiful sheet of water; for the sky, barred with crimson and purple, flooded the surface with its own deep hues, while Dog Mountain and Mount Mansell flung themselves darkly down at full length on the calm, pulseless tide. And out of their shadows loomed numerous spectral sails, while a light in the window of a distant cottage threw down a faint flame that vainly tried to dance upon the waves rising in our homeward track.

At half-past nine o'clock our boat grounded at the head of the sound, and soon after the kind hostess of the Mount Desert House welcomed me to a steaming supper.

# AMONG THE MOUNTAINS.

## CHAPTER VII.

Bar Harbor — The Ascent of Green — The Prospect — Night — A Thunder-Storm — The Descent — Newport — Homer — Round Peak — Echo Notch — Dry Mountain — Up Green — Back Again.

NOTWITHSTANDING the beauty of the western group, the mountains east of Somes' Sound present still greater interest and variety. Consequently they are better known, and more thoroughly studied.

With the exception of Mansell and Sargent, they are all to be reached from the east side of the sound. Bar Harbor is the proper point of departure, and by making the ascent of Newport and Green Mountain, we can gain an acquaintance with the rest.

Of all these sea-girt mountains, Newport, after Green Mountain, is deservedly the most popular. Some persons even place Newport in the advance of Green, declaring that it has peculiar attractions for which nothing can compensate. Yet, while conceding the advantages of Newport, Green Mountain elevates itself above all the rest, both in pictorial interest and in commanding height.

In crossing the island to Bar Harbor, our friend Oldstyle, and others averse to climbing, were left behind, while new friends and acquaintances entered the circle. Here the mountain tramp is never a solitary excursion. At a signal, troops of pedestrians issue forth to explore the neighboring regions, and two or three in nearly every circle were always ready to climb the highest peak and the most difficult pass

But happily Green Mountain presents few obstacles in the way of visitors. For a number of years the officers of the Coast Survey had an Observatory on its summit, and when work was suspended a tolerable road was left, which has since been improved to such an extent that carriages can, if necessary, ascend to the top; though it is the custom for most persons to perform the last two miles on foot. The whole distance, four miles from the village, is a pleasant excursion for a pedestrian in full strength.

As we ascend, Eagle Lake comes in view on the right, lying along the flank of the mountain in a trough-like depression, while beyond the ranges rise in regular order. The view towards Newport and the sea is shut in by the woody ridge of Green Mountain, along the back-bone of which the road runs, though at several points about half way up may be had charming glimpses of Goldsborough Mountains and Frenchman's Bay. Finally, on reaching the top, a glowing prospect greets the eye, land and sea mingling in the most captivating forms. In a clear day

the view is very extensive. Katahdin shows a clearly
defined peak many miles distant, while Mount Washington at times will even vouchsafe to unveil its
head.

On the ocean, Mount Desert Rock may be distinguished with the aid of a glass about fifteen miles
distant, while a maze of beautiful islands rise up
around the shores. The scene is one of great beauty.
Whittier gives a sketch in his poem of *Mogg Megone*,
placing his French hermit priest on one of these
peaks, where, while gazing on the scene below, he

" May half forget the dreams of home,
That nightly with his slumbers come,—
The tranquil skies of sunny France,
The peasant's harvest song and dance,
The vines around the hill-side wreathing,
The soft airs 'midst their clusters breathing,
The wing which dipped, the star that shone
Within thy bosom, blue Garonne.
&ast; &ast; &ast; &ast; &ast; &ast;
For here before him is unrolled,
Bathed deep in morning's flood of gold,
A vision gorgeous as the dream
Of the beatitudes may seem;
When as his Church's legends say,
Borne upward in extatic bliss,
The rapt enthusiast soars away
In a brighter world than this:
A mortal's glimpse beyond the pale—
A moment's lifting of the veil."

The top of Green Mountain is grooved out by two
little vallies which run nearly north-west and south-
east. The western valley, which descends towards the

sea, is filled with small trees and shrubs. Crossing near its head and descending in a westerly direction, we reach the brow, where may be had a fine view of the wild region lying between Green Mountain and Sargent. Pemetic is seen close at hand, lifting up its sharp barren ridge; the Bubble Mountains next appear, rejoicing modestly in their green crowns of lesser height; beyond is the dark but splendid range of Sargent, shutting in the sky; while Eagle Lake stretches northward at our feet. Only the more persistent climber penetrates into these recesses of Mount Desert, where he may any day come face to face with the fierce-looking but inoffensive wild-cat, or the harmless deer. One never tires of looking down upon the dark, tangled woods, the jagged peaks, and dusky glens, where the light and shade hold perpetual play, bringing out the strongest and most beautiful effects.

Other very fine views may be had, to see which we must scramble around the entire summit. But only one of these can be mentioned here, though in some respects it is the grandest to be had on the whole island. It is seen from the north-east brow, where the visitor looks down into the Otter Creek Valley, lying between Green Mountain and its spur known as Dry Mountain. The prospect is marked both by variety and magnitude. Immediately before us is the valley, a thousand feet deep, clothed in dark green forests, well-watered in the centre by a cool, invisible brook, and terminating in the blue fiord of Otter

Creek ; beyond is the ridge of Dry Mountain and the peak of Newport, rising in bold relief against the sea ; while to the left, far down upon the shore, is the village of Bar Harbor, fronting the isles and waters of Frenchman's Bay. Language cannot fitly convey an adequate impression of the beauty of this scene, which when once viewed will linger forever in the memory.

It was a beautiful July morning when we made our first excursion to the summit, in company with a merry party. Occasionally we saw the glacial marks on the rocks, that Agassiz views as records of the Ice-period in Maine ; but we were chiefly interested in the prospect, which unfolded some fresh charm at every step. On reaching the summit we were denied a view of the more distant objects, such as Katahdin and Mount Washington, which are seen only in re-markable clear weather, but objects far out at sea were distinctly visible. We enjoyed a beautiful sun-set, yet as night came on the fog rolled in from the sea, shutting out the view of the numerous beacon lights that twinkle on the coast. Only the light on Bear Island appeared at intervals.

The world below being wrapped in darkness, we were obliged to confine ourselves to the little house erected here for the entertainment of visitors. It is a rough-built structure, thrown together on the umbrella principle, with all the framework showing on the inside, being braced up without by light timbers of spruce planted in the rock to enable it to withstand the heavy gales. The little parlor in the centre is flanked by the dining-room, and a couple of dormitories, while overhead, in a loft, a double tier of berths is arranged, steamboat fashion, for the further accommodation of the disciples of Morpheus. During those cold, stormy nights which occur on the mountain even in the middle of July, the well-filled stove is no unwelcome companion, but tends to promote jollity in the circle of wayfarers usually gathered around it. Here, when supper is over, the adventures of the day are recited, the song is sung, and the story told, while the walls at times will crack with peals of laughter.

At an early hour the weary pedestrian usually retires, with a firm resolution to be up betimes and receive the first greetings of Old Sol as he rises from his ocean bed. Our company followed the custom of the place, though not before some young sons of Yale had executed a grand bear dance on the rough board floor in the loft which had been assigned to their use. Mine host looked slightly aghast when he heard the timbers groaning about his ears, but on being assured that the party was no less safe than noisy and "all right," he took a candle and sought his downy couch, simply enjoining us to put out the lights when we got ready.

The tired Collegians, however, had hardly ended their performance on the light fantastic toe, when a fearful thunder-storm arose, which set the sky all ablaze and made the mountains reel. When morning came no glorious sunrise greeted our eye, but the heavens were still pealing, while the lightning seemed fairly to rain down upon every part of the country below. It was one of those storms such as the inhabitant of Mount Desert experiences but once in a lifetime, being tropical both in its characteristics and disastrous effects.

When breakfast was over the storm abated, and we went forth to view as much of the prospect as could be discerned through the mist. The rain had fallen in floods, and the cascades were tearing over the rocks and shooting down the steep ledges, while the fog veiling Otter Creek Valley only occasionally opened and gave a glimpse of the half-drowned woods below.

Soon the most of the party grew weary of watching the fog, and all but two departed for Bar Harbor. By four o'clock in the afternoon my own patience was exhausted, and in the midst of a driving gale and blinding fog, Amarinta and I left the house, started down the deluged road, and pushed on without pausing, until at the end of an hour and a half we entered the hotel at Bar Harbor. Thus, for the time, ended our dreams of Green Mountain.

Several days after, while the ledges in the mountain were still glistening with mimic cascades, we ascended beautiful Newport, which from every point of view appears a perfect picture. In form, it is the most symmetrical of the mountains, while it has just verdure enough to set off its splendid cliffs to great advantage.

Just below the junction of the Otter Creek and Schooner-Head Roads, a cart-track leads away to the right towards the foot of Newport, terminating in a path, which turns to the left and runs up to the lowest ridge. Reaching this path, the climber makes his way upward. Soon the spur on the right, known as Round Peak, assumes a definite form, and the ocean appears on the left. Little cairns piled up at intervals now indicate the way.

An hour's climbing brought my two companions and myself to the highest peak, surmounted by a pyramid of stones. Here we took a brief rest and disposed of our lunch, which was washed down with liberal draughts of rain water found in the depressions of the rock, and, which being bitter, we called lichen broth. To sweeten such a vegetable compound would require the skill of a Moses. But even this beverage is found only after a rain, while of living springs there are none. My sentimental friend will say that these are carnalities, yet nothing adds less to the enjoyment of Newport than a hungry stomach, or a burning thirst.

One charm of Newport Mountain is found in its nearness to the ocean. Only a narrow strip of land intervenes between its base and the sea. From its summit we could look down upon the deck of a passing steamer, the Lewiston, sailing for South-west Harbor. The jagged drongs of Egg Rock were goring the breakers like so many mad bulls, while Schoodic Point and the coast of Maine lay shining in the sun. Elsewhere all was filled up by the restless waves.

Inland lay Green Mountain, covering the more distant heights with its huge bulk. My friend The Scholar, recently let loose from Yale, was fond of pocket editions of the classics; and on the way up he had labored to show us the resemblance of Homer's *Poluphloisboio Thalassas* to the voice of the loud-sounding sea. But now, as we lay under the shadow of the cairn, the *Iliad* was drawn forth from a side-pocket, where it had balanced the opposite luncheon-box, to perform a new service. The Scholar thought and herein we agreed with him, that one line conveyed admirably the characteristics of Mount Desert. Homer speaks of the "very many shadowy mountains and the resounding sea"; "And now," said The Scholar "just look at Green Mountain!" We enthusiastically applauded the idea. The old Bard photographs both the isles of Greece and Mount Desert heights.[1]

But a long tramp was before us, and we did not delay to view the two lesser peaks of Newport which break the long range in its descent to the sea at Otter

(1)—Οὐ γὰρ ἐγὼ Τρωων ἕνεκ᾽ ἤλυθον αἰχμητάων
δεῦρο μαχησόμενος· ἐπεὶ οὔτιμοι αἴτιοί εἰσιν.
οὐ γὰρ πώποτ᾽ ἐμὰς βοῦς ἤλασαν, οὐδὲ μὲν ἵππους,

Creek; nor to view "Loch Anna," a little body of
water named by Church, who saw it set like a diamond in the lower spur.   With regret we bade adieu
to this romantic height, where the earth and sky seem
so much in love with one another, and began the toilsome descent westward down over the steep cliffs and
through the pathless woods.   Finally we touched the
lower spur of Round Peak, and then pushed vigor-
ously on, until we struck the Otter Creek road, and
found ourselves in Echo Notch, which is walled in by
the steep sides of Dry Mountain.   Here, overshad-
owed by the towering cliffs, one almost fancies himself
in the White Mountain Notch.   In a calm day the
echo is splendid.   Some verses composed for *Lippin-
cott's Magazine* so well describe the place that they
may be given here :

> " Grim mountain Sprite! that, robed in woods,
>   Dost sit among these hills, their rightful King,
>   Forgive the wight who rashly dares
>   To vex thy silence with his questioning.

---

> οὐδέ ποτ' εν Φθίη ἐριβώλακι, βωτιανείρῃ,
> καρπὸν ἐδηλήσαντ'· ἐπείμάλα πολλ μεταξὺ
> οὐρεά τε σκιόεντα, θάλλασσά τε ἠχήεσσα.
>
> ILIAD, B. I., l. 152.

> Well dost thou know that 't was no feud of mine,
> With Troy's brave sons that brought me here in arms;
> They never did me wrong; they never drove
> My cattle or my horses; never sought
> In Phthia's fertile, life-sustaining fields,
> To waste the crops; for wide between us lay
> The shadowy mountains and the roaring sea.
>
> DERBY'S TRANSLATION.

Adown thy steep and rugged flanks
The black fir glooms and the pale aspens quiver.
And o'er thy glistening, wind-swept cliffs,
The mossy, perfumed streamlets leap forever.

We call to thee; our feeble cry
Dies 'gainst the rocky faces of thy throne;
And from the shaggy bosom comes
Thine answer, deep-voiced as an organ tone.

In that broad breast no human heart
To human pulses answereth again:
The wandering wretch, in wood-paths lost,
To thy stern face for pity looks in vain.

Within that Sphinx-like face we fain
Would read the riddle of life's fleeting story—
Thy calm eternal would we grasp,
And gild our gloom with thy far-shining glory.

But thou! Thou gazest on the sea,
With fir-crowned, stony brow that changes never:
We leave thee, in dumb mystery,
Dread Sprite! to heave that hoary bulk forever."

Our destination was the top of Green Mountain, and another scramble was inevitable. Therefore, without much delay, we struck through the pretty strip of wood skirting the foot of the eminence, found a narrow wooded ravine, and, keeping where we could take advantage of the trees, worked our way up. From the foot of the mountain we saw little more than what appeared an almost perpendicular granite wall, but we were gratified to find this convenient groove, though it was filled up with immense masses of fallen rocks, over which we were forced to climb. After an hour's labor we were finally able to overlook the peak of Newport and view the sea. In a quarter

of an hour more we were on the top of this spur,
called Dry Mountain, picking blueberries and seeking
for the best way across the ravine which separated us
from Green. We finally decided to take the most
shallow part of the ravine and push straight across.
At this place the mountain appears to have been split
in two, leaving the steep walls facing each other on
either hand. To get down the east side is nearly as
difficult as to get up the west, while at every step we
were in danger of dislodging huge masses of rock that
needed scarcely more than a finger's touch to send
them thundering below. Where the operation was
safe we found it capital sport, but prudence taught us
on these occasions to keep close together, lest some
flying boulder should sweep one of us into the black
ravine. At the bottom is a dense forest of spruce and
fir ; and among the loose rocks, covered in some places
to the depth of nearly a foot with soft, green, spongy
moss, was a small, ice-cold stream, tinkling musically
on its way to Otter Creek. In this shady chasm,

> " An hydeous hole al vaste, withouten shape,
>     Of endless deph, orewhelmde with ragged stone,"

the atmosphere was as frigid as the water, and, with
chattering teeth, we again sought the soft summer air.
But now we found the hardest climb of all. The
Scholar, quite forgetting Homer and the " shadowy
mountains," flung his stalwart frame against the iron
cliffs and gave us a splendid illustration of muscular

Christianity, while our legal friend, erst a crack oars-
man of Yale, and tough as steel. made an equally
powerful demonstration ; but the slippery rocks were
at times perfectly inexorable, and we were frequently
forced to climb the trees and swing ourselves up.
Finally, we surmounted this tremendous barrier, and,
gasping for breath, sat down to rest.

But -the sunset view from the summit was still
before us, and we soon hastened up along the ledges
towards the Green Mountain House, delaying however, at the right point for a parting glance at Otter
Creek Valley, which was fast filling up with the
sombre shade.

As we neared the house, mine Host appeared from
behind the wood-pile with an armful of sticks. We
bade him hail, and bespoke a fire, which was soon
crackling in the stove, adding much to our comfort.
Supper likewise tended to put us in a mood to enjoy
the evening pyrotechnics of Old Sol, and while he was
preparing to draw the bright curtains of the clouds
around him and plunge out of sight, we took our sticks
and wearily began the trudge down the rough mountain road. This journey is one that always repays
the investment of muscle, though it is never more
enjoyable than at the evening hour. How beautifully
does the prospect unfold itself! Eagle Lake shim-
mering in the golden light, the birds-eye view of
Somes' Sound and Blue Hill, the dismantled, half-
spectral pines, Sargent's gray and dusky sides, num-

berless green valleys and lesser hill-tops, and the
islanded and purpling waters of Frenchman's Bay—
all these combine to form a most enchanting picture
which assumes new combinations and produces exquisite effects at every turn in the winding road.
Along the lower slopes, however, the daylight disappeared, and through the opening in the woods we saw
the stars being slowly lighted up ; while the night-
hawks circled around our heads, uttering what at this
hour always seems such a mournful cry.  Bringing
off as I did a heavy sprain as a souvenir of the tramp,
I gave way slightly to the influences of the hour and
walked on in silence at a little distance behind my
friends, whom I heard discussing all sorts of subjects,
beginning with " Culprit Fay," and ending with the
respective merits of Theology and Law.  The disciple
of Blackstone stoutly averred that the Law made
men remarkably exact, while Theology tended to
looseness, there being no opposition counsel in court
to pick him in pieces.  Of course his view was duly
refuted ; though for my own part I thought that both
were about half right.  I mention this simply to show
the turn which thought often takes here, the morning
fancy often ending in questions of fact.  Two hours
after sunset we reached home.

Next to Green Mountain, on the west, is Pemetic,
so called for the purpose of perpetuating the Indian
name of Mount Desert.  It extends south-eastwardly

from the end of Eagle Lake, and gradually sinks down towards the sea, presenting a sharp granite ridge, which, when viewed from the north, fairly cleaves the sky. It may be reached from Bar Harbor by the way of the Otter Creek road, yet the journey is too long. The short route is to ascend Eagle Lake and climb its steep side. Landing on one of the two white sand beaches at the head of the lake, we struck into the woods, keeping just within the border of the old forest, as the recent growth is well nigh impassable, on account of the dense thickets.

Glancing at the mountain, we concluded that half an hour would be sufficient to take us to the top. Yet we were greatly disappointed, erring both in regard to the height to be climbed and the difficulties to be encountered. The fallen timber disputed our progress at nearly every step, while for about three quarters of an hour the summit continued to recede. Still we scrambled on, and, after getting clear of the woods, made our way from ledge to ledge, until we stood upon the topmost of the series, which terminate on the east side in perpendicular walls.

Nearly an hour and a half was consumed in reaching the summit of Pemetic, which is both grand and bare. It is sufficiently high to afford a glimpse of the Green Mountain House on the east, and a full view of the recesses of Sargent and the Bubble Mountains. Northward is the lake, and more distant the region around Trenton Bridge, while southward is a superb

view of the islands and the sea. The islands probably appear to better advantage from this point than
any other. On Green Mountain the tourist is too far
above them and the details are lost; but here the
floating masses of pale green assume a definite character, and profitably employ the eye.

Still what most impressed us was the wildness of
the scene. The upper portion of Pemetic is a mass
of rose-colored granite descending eastward in a
series of long gigantic steps; while the half-covered
sides of Green Mountain combine with the positive
desolation of Sargent to complete the rugged character of the view and fill it with romantic interest.
Jordan's Pond also adds an important feature, lying
cradled under the cliffs of Sargent, dark, and threatening, and appearing altogether as if it would like to
drown one. This is a splendid place in which to pass
the day, or to camp at night, while to the artist or
photographer it is worth a fortune.

The deer are still found in the mountains. Last
summer a Harvard student found a pair of antlers
on Pemetic. As is well known, they shed them
every year, at least until they reach old age; which is
the case with the moose, who throws off antlers weigh-
ing from twenty-five to fifty pounds as easily as a Jew
puts off "old clo'." The deer swim off to the island
from the main-land every fall to escape the dogs that
are set to driving them out of the woods. Forty
years ago, I am told, the deer were strangers to the

place; and if the hunting were stopped in the neighboring regions they would soon disappear from the
island. But, as it is, fresh stock comes on every
autumn. The Oldtown Indians resort here every
season to hunt them, in connection with the otter, fox,
wild-cat, muskrat, and mink. The law allows the
deer to be hunted for three months, ending with the
fifteenth of December. In coming here the Indians
simply followed the custom of their ancestors. The
old chroniclers occasionally mention their visits, as
is the case with Hubbard, who connects it with the
captivity of young Cobett, son of the minister at
Ipswich, Massachusetts, who was taken prisoner by
the Indians, near Portland, in 1677. He was afterwards taken by his "pateroon," or master, to Mount
Desert, where he was accustomed to spend his winters,
and arrange his hunting expeditions. Hubbard says :
" In that desert-like condition was the poor young
man forced to continue nine weeks in the service of a
savage miscreant, who sometimes would tyrannize over
him, because he could not understand his language,
and for want thereof might occasion him to miss his
game, or the like." At the end of nine weeks "on a
sudden he took a resolution to send this young man
down to Penobscot to Mr. [Baron] Casteen to pro-
cure more powder to kill moose and deer, which it
seems is all their way of living at Mount Desert."
This journey led to his ransom, which was finally
effected by being exchanged for a good coat. Hub-

bard tells us how that on one occasion while a prisoner on the island he went out to hunt, and was so
overcome by the cold that he became senseless, and
that the Indians were obliged to take him on their
shoulders and carry him to the nearest wigwam.
Formerly, also, the beaver was plenty here, as is still
attested by the remains of their dams.

Between Pemetic and Sargent lie the Bubble Mountains, or Twins. The larger of the two heights stands
at the head, or north end of Jordan's Pond, and the
other advances along the eastern side. They form
the two principal peaks of a ridge lying on the west
side of Eagle Lake. Between this ridge and Sargent's Mountain is a narrow valley rising at its northern extremity even with the lesser elevation, and
furnishing an additional water-shed to Jordan's Pond.
The whole region between Eagle Lake and Sargent's
Mountain is covered with a dense forest of somewhat
recent growth that effectually bars every approach to
The Twins.

One day we made a party to climb them, and
started from Bar Harbor at nine o'clock in the morning. Walking to Eagle Lake, we found the boats all
out, and therefore tried to find our way through the
woods, beating about among the bushes until high
noon. At this time we gave up the attempt and
divided, one party striking out westward to scale Sargent's Mountain and return home by Jordan's Pond

and the Otter Creek road, while the other returned to the McFarland House to form some new plan. There I drove a hard bargain for a boat which was just returning down the lake, stipulating that when done with it should be left on the beach at the other end, from whence the owner should bring it home again at his convenience. At half past two o'clock we got into the boat and rowed up the lake against a heavy breeze and a short, chop sea, which severely taxed our strength. Landing at last on the farthest sand beach, we crossed the creek to the west, and struck up the steep side of the Bubble ridge, keeping well to the right, and touched the top after a lively scramble of twenty minutes. Starting from thence in a southerly direction through trees and underwood, ten minutes more brought us to the highest point, when the object of the expedition was declared accomplished. And the result amply repaid us for all the toil of the day, affording as it did some of the grandest views, besides an accurate knowledge of the geography of this part of the island. Westward, and far above us, lay Sargent's Mountain, holding up to our gaze its torn and rifted sides; to the north stretched what we may call the Valley of The Twins; on the east the forest cut off the prospect of Eagle Lake, while southward lay Jordan's Pond and the islands out at sea.

As we sat gazing upon the summit of Sargent, our friends whom we had left in the woods appeared in the form of two dark specks, moving along the ridge against the evening sky. One was a Harvard College undergraduate, who, the year before, rowed his wherry from Boston to Mount Desert. They had fought their way through the thickets to the top of Sargent, and were now taking a fifteen mile walk home. Quickly arranging a signal with our pocket handkerchiefs, we hoisted it on a pole, and gave a united shout. The signal was recognized, and the sound of our voices, aided by the wind, also succeeded in getting across the great gulf that separated us, and then crept up to Sargent's ridge. A faint balloo came back in reply, and then, after viewing one another for some time, we started homeward by opposite routes, our own covering as good as a dozen miles. Of the distance separating the two peaks we could form no estimate. The voice of the sentinel has been heard sounding the "All's well" from Old to New Gibraltar, a distance of nine miles; yet our own voices probably did not reach half as far.

On our return we paused a few minutes at the brink of the cliffs overlooking Eagle Lake to enjoy the beauty of the prospect here spread out before us, it being an exquisite mingling of lake, mountain, and forest, and then cautiously descended to the strand. We embarked, rowed to the Eastern shore, beached the boat, and then struck through the low ground which here skirts the foot of Green Mountain; afterwards going up its steep sides and reaching the top in an hour and a quarter. Arriving at the Moun-

tain House we found a company duly assembled
around the August fire, intending to stay over night.
But as it was already sunset we bade mine Host good
evening, started homeward by the road, and arrived
at Bar Harbor in an hour and twenty minutes. I
mention the time made for the benefit of those climbers
in whose hands this book may fall.

It now only remains to speak of Kebo—little Kebo
—sitting at the foot of Green Mountain, like some
scholar at the feet of his master, and modestly rejoicing in its green prime. Many persons who have travelled far and near in Mount Desert may perhaps have
never seen this hill, which is set away almost out of
sight. Yet the walk to Kebo is one of the most
enjoyable on the island. Indeed, after being surfeited
with the grandeur of rugged rocks and tremendous
precipices the tranquil beauty that surrounds Kebo is
hailed as a welcome relief.

Taking the Green Mountain road as far as the
cross-road at the school-house, and turning to the left,
half an hour's walk from Bar Harbor brings us to the
place where we gain the best view of Kebo. The
view here is one of great loveliness, and some even,
after seeing every other part of the island, have not
hesitated to pronounce it the best of all. This,
however, is because nothing in particular is generally
expected, and the picture forms a pleasant surprise.
There at the border of the fields rises this little hill,

with its perpendicular eastern face, while beyond are
Newport, Round Peak, Dry, and Green Mountains.
All now appear verdure-clad to their very summits.
Between Dry and Newport is Echo Notch, through
which we can look, and at the same time have a view
of the ravine which sweeps down from between Dry
and Green Mountains.   From this point we continue
on past a couple of farm-houses until we reach a picturesque old mill, when, if we desire to climb Kebo,
we must cross the stream, turn up the wood-road to
the right, and follow on until the west side is gained,
from whence the ascent is easily made.   No path will
be found until near the top, nor is one really needed,
since there are so few obstacles in the way.   Half or
three quarters of an hour will bring the slowest
walkers thither, where the most lovely panorama is
spread out.   Kebo has an elevation of not more than
three or four hundred feet, but here we realize once
more that there is no necessary connection between
height and beauty.   Here, too, in the favorable light,
the whole region appeared clothed in living green.
Even the dry Porcupines out in Frenchman's Bay,
which at noon-day usually wear a barren aspect, now
glowed with a deep emerald light, and the face of
nature was everywhere wreathed in smiles.   From
this position the structure of Kebo also becomes apparent, and it is found to be a ridge with two well-
defined peaks running parallel with Green and fading
away on the side of Dry Mountain   Between Kebo

and Green is a broad and beautiful valley ; while east of the former elevation runs a bow-shaped ridge, bending westward, and reaching from the gateway of Echo Notch to the cross-road already mentioned. This ridge, marked on the map as The Gate of the Notch, is quite high and flat at its southern end, and when seen from Frenchman's Bay it seems to lie directly across the entrance to this splendid vale ; yet in walking to Otter Creek the pedestrian will find that the Gate conveniently stands ajar.

In returning from Kebo, we tried to descend the cliffs on the east side, but were forced to give it up, the sheer, rocky walls being too much for us. We accordingly retraced our steps. In the fields we found Agricola, raking hay, and asked what amount of filthy lucre would induce him to give us the exclusive possession of his little pastoral paradise next season. This enchanted isle, with all its sweet nooks and romantic corners, could furnish nothing better for a summer home. With little Kebo, we bid the mountains adieu.

# *THE LAKE REGION.*

## CHAPTER VIII.

LAKES like those of Mount Desert cannot
fail to excite admiration. Beautiful in
themselves, they give to the surrounding
region as much as they receive. They
are not all dignified by the name of lake, several
being known simply as ponds. Three of these sparkling sheets of water lie on each side of Somes'
Sound.

The most western is known as Seal Cove Pond.
It lies on the north-east of Western Mountain and
empties into Seal Cove. It is about four miles in
length, and in its broadest part about a fourth of a
mile in width. A dam at the lower end prevents the
salt water from flowing in, while the fresh water does
good service at the mill as it flows out. The ride
from South-west Harbor to Seal Cove has many
attractions. The distance is about five miles, and in.
reaching the lake it is necessary to go completely
around the spur of Western Mountain. The cove

was famous in former times as the resort of seals. At present it is a snug harbor for small craft, numbers of which are built here. At the head of the cove a high bridge is crossed, and, turning to the right, the lake comes in full view. At this place there are a few houses, yet the general appearance of things is rather sleepy. There is good fishing to be had, and trout and perch are usually ready for the hook. But we did not delay to test their appetite, nor even to row on the lake, as the clouds seemed to promise rain. The water looked somewhat dark, and around the shore the vegetation indicated that it was shallow, though in the central portions it is deep enough. At the head of the lake is a pond which serves as a sort of feeder. In passing on to Somesville we noticed but few dwellings, though we saw no less than two meeting-houses with their roofs falling in. Formerly they were occupied by Baptists, but on inquiry we learned that the religious interest formerly felt had greatly declined.

Before reaching Somesville, charming views were gained of the waters of the north shore of the island towards Trenton Bridge. The outlet of Long Lake was also seen as we passed. The water at this point runs toward the sound, and, owing to the operations of the mill, savored somewhat of the character of a saw-dust soup.

In going from Somesville to South-west Harbor on what is called the Pretty-marsh Road, we had a fine

opportunity for observing Denning's Lake, which is
about four miles long.  For a couple of miles the road
runs nearly along its shore, and the view is unobstructed by foliage.  This lake boasts a single island.
On the opposite side the long slope of Beech Mountain rises in its own peculiar beauty.  As we go
southward, the road gradually ascends along the base
of Dog Mountain, while at the head of this lake Beech
Mountain suddenly shoots up into the air, presenting
that immense precipice known as Storm Cliff, and of
which mention has already been made.  In the bright-
est weather it wears a threatening aspect, and seems
to frown.  The wall of *debris* accumulated here at
the foot of the cliff, descends rapidly to the deep water,
which lies dark and sullen in the shade.  This ram-
part of rock, lifting itself up into the sky, looks as if it
would last forever, yet the unseen, but acting powers
of the air are busily at work flinging down fragment
on fragment, and the time may eventually come when
the deep water on its front will not float a boat.  The
expression of the lake at this point is grand.  Words
cannot convey a just sense of its impressive character.

In visiting these two lakes we complete a circle,
still leaving Long Lake, which lies between them, to
be examined.  The distance from South-west Harbor is about two and a half miles, by the Beech
Mountain road, from which we finally diverge towards the westward, or left, and again at the proper
distance, to the right.  This lake is totally unlike, and

has no connection with, the other two. It is situated
in a long deep valley, or trough, between Beech and
Western Mountains, which at the south end of the
lake rises gracefully upward on either hand, like the
inner side of a ship's walls, clothed with verdure to
the top. We descend to its margin by a rough wood-
road, gaining through the openings in the trees an
occasional glimpse of the water, which, in a clear day,
borrows its color, tone and expression from the skies;
yet, at certain hours, the woody mountains photograph
their green forms on its face.

The forest comes down to the edge of the water,
except at the end, where there is a beautiful beach,
drawn in the form of a bow, and covered with handsome granite pebbles. Here is found a lovely spot
either for pic-nic occasions or solitary hours. The
lake at this point is not broad, and a projecting spur
denies an extensive view; yet this circumstance pre-
pares the way for a pleasing surprise, when we get
fairly launched in a boat. Descending the lake, the
prospect opens until we look down the watery vista to
the end. The beauty nowhere rises into grandeur, as
at Denning's Lake, yet we find ourselves in a kind of
picture-gallery, where an artist might profitably spend
a week imbibing the pure lessons of nature.

When at Bar Harbor every person should improve
the occasion to visit Eagle Lake and Jordan's Pond.
The latter sheet of water may be reached from South-
west Harbor, by crossing Somes' Sound, and in going

by this route a view may be had of Hadlock's Pond;
yet most persons will find it quite as satisfactory to
take their departure from the opposite side of the
island, for the reason that this route requires the
employment of only one mode of travel.

Hadlock's Pond has some attractions, being composed of two bodies of water connected by an apology
for a creek, over which the road to North-east Harbor
passes, but it does not demand a special visit. Jordan's Pond, however, will well repay the journey of
about nine miles from Bar Harbor. The route lies
by the way of Echo Notch and Otter Creek. About
three miles beyond the latter place, the road to Jordan's touches the main road, turning back from it at a
sharp angle, and running northward for the distance
of a mile to the Jordan farm-house, which stands near
the outlet of the lake. This is the only dwelling
found here. Attached is a barn and some outbuild-
ings that have felt the hand of time. The situation is
solitary, but it is one of much beauty, and is capable
of great improvement as a place of resort. A short
walk through the fields terminates at the outlet of the
lake, marked by a dam and the skeleton of a mill.
The lake, for this is too fine a body of water to call a
*pond*, is about two miles long, and about half a mile
wide, lying between the southern spur of Sargent's
Mountain and Pemetic, with the Bubble Mountains,
or Twins, at its head. The eastern face of Sargent
looks toward the lake, which, according to the fashion

of these mountains, gives a long line of splendid cliffs, rising magnificently against the sky, a sort of Titanic wall. Pemetic looks across the lake at his neighbor, appearing grand and gray; while the Twins sit side side by side at the north, alike clad, as is meet, in robes of living green.

It was noon-tide when we reached the lake, where, among the rocks on the shore, the *cuisine* was set up and a fire put to crackling under a borrowed kettle, which was supported by a pine crotch. Amarinta pronounced the coffee prime; and when lunch was over we launched an old dory for the purpose of going on a voyage. But our plans were doomed to perish, for no sooner did the dory touch the lake than the water spurted up through a hundred holes. Thereupon Piscator cut a birch rod, produced his instruments of torture, and went off to inveigle the hapless trout. Disappearing among the bushes bordering the stream, he was seen no more until, in answer to our halloos, he left his rod and came forth to go home, having a string of fish in his hand for to-morrow's breakfast.

As for the rest of us, we lounged away the whole afternoon on the shore of the lake, saying, among other things, how fine it would be to push through the dense underwood skirting the feet of Sargent and scale the cliffs. We contented ourselves, however, with words.

It was interesting here to note the changes that

gradually took place on the lake. As the afternoon wore on and the slanting shadows were developing on the sides of the Twins, we found, as was also the case when we afterwards climbed them, that they did not stand side by side, but that one was pushed far in advance of the other, making out on the eastern side of the lake.

Towards six o'clock it began to grow damp and misty, and the fog gathered around the Twins, which caused one of the party to suggest that they were putting on their cloaks, preparatory to a general meet of the mountains. So we thought that we had better be going too. Therefore, after looking into the old farm-house, to see a man with only one leg, competing with the Lowell looms in the manufacture of cotton flannel, for weaving which he received ten cents a yard, we packed into our carriage,—an open one,—and drove off. Soon we had a pouring rain, with lightning and thunder, but Piscator drove up hill and down like mad, and brought us to Bar Harbor in less than two hours.

The last of the lakes to be mentioned is Eagle Lake, so called by Church, who sketched at Mount Desert during a number of summers. It stands higher above the sea than the other lakes, and is only two and a half miles from Bar Harbor. The outlet is found in a depression of the road half a mile beyond the foot of Green Mountain, and will be recognized by the frame of an old mill, which formerly made the water do some hard work. Of late years the mill interests in this region have been in a poor condition.

A short path through the bushes brings us to the shore of the lake, from whence the view up to its head is unobstructed. The lake in its general characteristics is bright and beautiful. It can hardly be said to possess the element of grandeur, under any circumstances, yet artists will perhaps find that it has more material for pictures than any other in the island. It is about two miles long, and of tolerable openness at the sides, while the country towards the north is sufficiently low to afford distant views of the nearest mainland. On the east side are the flanks of Green Mountain, sweeping gradually up towards the apex, and on the west is the low ridge running north from the sides of the Twins, while still farther west is seen the huge form of Sargent, its bold peak towering upward to the sky. At the south end the aspect of Pemetic is remarkably beautiful and bold. Starting near the east side of the lake, its ridge runs diagonally away towards the south-east, the top being sharp and rounded like the edge of an upturned hatchet. Without even a human being, the scene, especially when the lake is ruffled, seems full of life. So great is the variety, that even the solitary boatman seldom feels alone.

But as regards boats the lakes of Mount Desert are not particularly well provided, and it will often be found necessary to employ some wretched hulk, unless careful provision is made by an arrangement in advance. In the account of Bubble Mountain I spoke of rowing up the lake, but on another occasion I was not fortunate in securing a good boat, and Theologicus and myself were obliged to go up to Pemetic in an old leaky yawl, bedaubed with tar, with short pieces of board for oars. It was a beautiful afternoon, however, and a light breeze from the north favored us, so that we paddled thoughtlessly up the lake, not thinking how we should get back. As we passed the cliffs in the Bubble ridge, they seemed to come forward towards the water to look down upon us, and then gradually withdraw from sight. Towards the upper end they are between three and four hundred feet high, and crowned with plumes of pine. In one place the birches are so intermingled with the arbor vitæ, that it is impossible to go through without a sharp axe. At this end is a number of beautiful sand beaches, on one of which I found the track of deer. There are plenty of lake trout to be had, though of other kinds of fish there are none. I was here told of a great water-snake which formerly made its habitation in the lake. The story goes, that in a fire, which burned the woods, he was overtaken and broiled alive. I afterwards found that the story had travelled as far as Grand Menan, and the reader may be assured that it lost nothing in the passage. At that place I met a Lubec fisherman formerly acquainted with this island. He was profoundly superstitious, and no marvel was too great for his faith. Everything in the shape of a wonderful story was seized with eagerness, and he would dwell upon ghosts with apparent delight. The people of New Brunswick were just then excited about the sea-serpent seen in Lake Utopia, the accounts of which, together with the preparations for his capture, filled several columns in the public journals. For my own part I was sceptical, and all the arguments of our friend the fisherman did not avail. Finally, a bright idea seemed to enter his mind, and he broke as follows :

" Say, now, ain't you from Mount Desert ?"

" Yes."

" Wall, they had one *there*, any how."

" But that, according to the affidavit, sworn to in court, was seen fourteen miles away from the land."

" 'Shaw, *that* ain't it. You've come all the way from Mount Desert and ain't heern tell on 'im. He was n't *in* the sea. Now you know that mighty pooty pond up by Green Mountain ?"

" Yes."

" Wall, that's the place where the sarpint was. He'd come right out of the pond and ketch a lamb an' eat 'im, and they couldn't do nothing, cos he was so big. But the woods got afire and killed 'im, and when they found 'im there wus forty jints of backbone a foot thick."

" Ah," was the somewhat incredulous rejoinder.

" Don't b'lieve it, hey ?   Wall, then, *I've seed 'em !*"

This triumphant declaration, made in a tone indicating the consciousness of victory, was accompanied by an emphatic slap on his knee with a hand nearly as broad as one of his own salt mackerel.   Furthermore, I might see one of these bones myself at Bass Harbor, on my return.   I, of course, promised so to do, at the same time putting down the name of the possessor of this remarkable but neglected relic, which would be sufficient to gladden the heart of Storer or Agassiz for a whole month.

But I forgot that Theologicus and myself were just now on Eagle Lake, that " mighty pooty pond," from which we did not escape so easily.   Reaching the last sand-beach we climbed Pemetic.   On looking around for water to quench our thirst, we found it was altogether unlike Homer's Ida, " abundant in springs," and were forced to accept a draft of lichen soup from a crevice in the rock.   While here my mind recurred to a passage in Dr. Johnson's account of his tour to the western islands of Scotland.   Being at one place by ease and choice, and with no immediate evil to fear, he nevertheless says, that " the imaginations excited by an unknown and untravelled wilderness, are not such as arise in the artificial solitude of parks and gardens,—a flattering notion of self-sufficiency, a placid indulgence of voluntary delusions, a secure expansion of the fancy, or a cool concentration of the mental powers.   The phantoms that haunt a desert are want, and misery, and danger; the evils of dereliction rush upon the thoughts; man is made unwillingly acquainted with his own weakness, and meditation shows him how little he can sustain and how little he can perform." The force of these observations will always be felt by thoughtful minds when climbing among the slippery cliffs that look down in solemn grandeur upon the lakes of Mount Desert, but I hardly agree with him about the effect of such situations upon the fancy; for the unwieldy philosopher, treading like some elephant among the rocks of Mull, was timid, and therefore not qualified to stand, in this respect, as the representative man.

We lingered here until the mountain peaks around us were burnished by the rays of the setting sun, when we were favored with an unusually fine exhibition in the west, the rich golden glow being healthy in its tone, and altogether unlike those green-sick yellows which Bierstadt sometimes forces to the jaundice point.

At the last moment we began to stumble down the mountain amid the deepening twilight. This task occupied more than an hour. Finally we gained the boat, bailed her out, and, having no friendly breeze to carry us back, we were obliged to use our bits of board. These would have availed us nothing, if there had been a contrary wind. As it turned out, however, we had a beautiful, calm starlight night, and were able to paddle slowly down the lake. The echoes

among the mountains on this occasion proved remarkably fine, the sound of our voices being returned from
all quarters.  So we cheerfully paddled on, only stopping occasionally to talk with the hills, or to bail out
the boat which leaked like a sieve.  In the course of
the evening the moon rose from behind a cloud, and
once looked out upon the lake.  But gentle Luna
seemed far from pleased with the prospect, and with-
drew her face.

It was past ten o'clock when we approached the
landing at the foot of the lake.  At a little hut on the
shore of a cove, a Harvard student and his friend
were passing the night, in order to be on hand for the
trout by daylight in the morning.  We heard them
singing college songs at the top of their voices, uncon-
scious of the fact that they had an audience.  In the
afternoon they saw us paddling down the lake, but, not
seeing us return, they concluded that we had left our
boat and gone over the mountains.  Unable, in the
darkness, to find the landing, we hailed them, and in
reply were invited ashore to the shanty, "to take
something," "some hot coffee."  But our heavy yawl
was afoul of the sunken rocks, and we therefore declined their invitation, and requested a pilot instead.
In a minute or two their little white boat, scarcely
more than a skiff, shot out from the dark cove like a
spectre, and after considerable trouble we were helped
in to the only piece of beach found here among the
boulders, and got ashore.  Just then the moon burst

out from among the clouds, flooding the pathway through the woods with a clear silver light. We accordingly bade our benefactors good night, and wearily began to plod the homeward way. At the distance of a mile and a half from Bar Harbor, we met the advance guard of an alarmed party coming out to the lake to search for us.

## BEACH RAMBLES.

### CHAPTER IX.

BEACH rambles at Mount Desert are invested with unusual interest, both by the splendid cliffs and caves, and by the immense tidal flow, which at the ebb lays bare the rocks and flats, unveiling a thousand secrets of the sea. Here the naturalist will find that a morning's walk is worth something. If really in earnest, he has only to step into a pair of long rubber boots, walk down to the shore, and, staff in hand, follow the receding waves. Among the rock-pools and shallows he will thus be able to explore the crystal dwellings of a large variety of marine creatures, and call upon, at their own homes, those marvels of ocean life that, farther south on the New England coast, might never be seen at all.

It is exceedingly interesting to inspect the huge star-fish and the monster anemone, whose outspread tentacles would fill a Derby hat; but, not everyone is willing to accept the invitation of the sea-side *savant*, who says, in the language of Caliban, " I prithee, let me bring thee where crabs grow." Most persons prefer to keep tolerably near the high water mark.

One of the most interesting localities for a beach ramble on the southern part of the island is at the Sea Wall, which is nothing less than the geologist's shingle beach. It appears almost as if built by human hands for a breakwater, a purpose that it indeed serves ; and yet a Cyclop would be unequal to the task accomplished by the waves. From the Ocean House, opposite the steamboat wharf at Southwest Harbor, to the sea wall, is just a fair half-hour's walk by a good road. On this road, too, may be had some beautiful views of the entire mountain region that can hardly be surpassed anywhere on the island. Still, as we are supposed to be out for a *beach* ramble, it may prove as well to cross the fields to the shore. Here the prospect is also fine, the entire eastern group being in sight, while northward we look up Somes' Sound. The entire walk around to the Sea Wall is full of interest. The way is rough and liberally strewn with boulders, but the scene is animated, and the gossip with the fisher-folk on the shore is not without profit. The afternoon when I walked that way the weather was fine, the breeze mild, and only a light swell falling with a gentle lush upon the shore. The most of the boats had come in, and the men were cleaning fish, or mending their nets. Blue-eyed children were playing around the beach, some still waiting for their fathers to come ashore. The fisherman's life is a hard one, and his family suffer much anxiety, notwithstanding their familiarity with the sea. I noticed a young woman leading a couple of children and walking up and down the beach. Erelong she went and sat on the bank, all the while looking earnestly seaward, straining her eyes to discover some object. She was waiting for her husband. Finally a well-known sail hove in sight around Cranberry Island, and came gliding on towards the beach, assisted by a leeward oar. When within hail, I heard her ask, " What luck, John ?" The individual thus laconically addressed, and whose head was surmounted by an old battered " sou'wester," replied by going to the sheets and hauling part way out of the water a huge halibut that he was towing astern. The answer was satisfactory, at least so said the wife's face; and now, gentle reader, wish them ever good luck, for,

> " O well may the boatie row,
> And better may she speed,
> And muckle luck attend the boat
> That wins the barnie's bread."

As I went on I thought of the fisher-women of Venice, who go to the shore of the Adriatic and sing a melody until they hear the voices of their returning husbands chaunting a reply.

Coming around the point upon the south shore, the Sea Wall appeared in sight, a broad and high ridge, composed of loose boulders varying in size from a loaf of bread to a barrel, with the ocean rolling in on one side and a low meadow on the other. The material is thrown up in great confusion, and persons unaccustomed to such sights are invariably impressed by its magnitude. At this point the rock underlying the whole island is exposed to the ravages of the sea, which breaks off large blocks, tossing them in the surf until some great storm comes, when the fragments are driven up beyond the ordinary line of operation to lie at rest.

This place is somewhat celebrated for the fine specimens of green feldspar usually obtainable. The mineral occurs in masses of various sizes, distributed generally among the rocks. Specimens are valued as souvenirs of the island. It is of a beautiful hue, though possessing all the characteristics of the ordinary feldspar. But notwithstanding its friable nature it has been successfully worked in the manufacture of ornaments. This is an excellent place to collect sea-mosses. Opposite are the Cranberry Islands, on one of which is seen a church spire. Dead Man's Beach may also be seen. It is so called for the reason that, long ago, a whole ship's crew was drowned there and buried in one common grave. On the Sea Wall wrecks are not infrequent, and the bones of one vessel were still lying where they had been tossed above high water mark. There is little hope of a ship that gets nipped in this place, for she is tolerably sure of being ground to pieces.

There are other spots on this part of the island well
worthy of being sought out, such, for instance, as Bass
Harbor and the east side of Clark's Point.  At the
latter place a ramble may be had along the sound.
Exploring in that vicinity one day, we found a hermit,
who has lived for about ten years on the point of land
opposite and close by Fernald's Point.  He is of the
same faith as the Jesuit Fathers who founded their
Mission within a few rods of his hut in 1613, yet very
unlike them in works.  Hearing by accident of his
existence, we resolved to pay him a visit, expecting to
find one of those venerable characters seen in old pictures, with flowing robes, sandaled feet, and a snowy
beard sweeping down his breast,

> " Like Barbarossa, who sits in his cave,
>    Taciturn, sombre, sedate and grave."

But instead, he proved a short, red-faced individual,
clad in a flannel shirt and patched, sordid trowsers,
with the remnant of a greasy felt hat on his head.
His house was a mere hut, about twenty feet square
and eight feet high, the flat roof having just enough
inclination to shed water.  The only mode of ingress
was through a latticed hen-coop, the roof of which
was partially formed of an old boat turned bottom up.
On invitation, we entered by this porch, and when the
pupils of our eyes had accommodated themselves to
the feeble light struggling in through a single pane
of glass, the situation became apparent.  Of floor

there was none, save the mother earth. On one side was a bunk for sleeping, and in the corner a bin for potatoes, with an old broken stove in the middle. All was wretched and unclean to the last degree, yet he seemed to feel very comfortable. He was also in good spirits, having just received five dollars from an artist for sitting for his portrait.

A glance into the bin discovered a sitting hen spreading herself, as the hermit said, over a dozen and a half of eggs, while in the corner another venerable fowl clucked proudly in the midst of fourteen offspring that had just walked out of their shells. When we begged for a little more light on the subject, he drew back a shingle slide underneath the pane of glass and revealed a hole which he said was for the accommodation of his cat. Looking into a corner the eyes of Felis appeared flashing in the twilight like a couple of balls of green fire. Getting out again we sat down on a bench, and listened to the hermit as he told his manner of life, passed so democratically in his dingy den with his chickens and cat. He was weary of the world, and liked to be with himself. His summer work secured the winter's simple fare. What wood he wanted the sympathizing waves tossed up at his door, and as for candle he had none. The long evenings were specially consecrate to meditation, spiritual songs and prayer. All this was for the good of his soul.

Amarinta hinted that cleanliness was next to godliness, which sentiment gave this disciple of St. Francis so little concern, that it was followed up with a pointed homily on dirt. For this likewise the holy man did not seem to care either, and when bringing some water he still had the courage to present a cup which Amarinta vainly turned around once and again in the endeavor to find the clean side.

In striking contrast with his hut and person was his "garden," yclept a potato patch, without weeds, faultlessly neat, inclosed by a brushwood fence, and extending to the edge of the beach. From thence he volunteered to bring Amarinta a "nosegay," but finally presented only a sprig of mint, of which he planted a little for "sickness." Aureole, who is a judge, afterwards vowed it was for juleps, and cited in proof the hermit's red nose. We bade the hermit of Mount Desert good day, persuaded that we had at least found a character.

Still, the great beach rambles are to be had on the east and south-east sides of the island. Bar Harbor must be the starting-point for all those localities. To reach Bar Harbor by land from South-west Harbor, we first drive to Somesville, and then, turning the head of the Sound, continue on eight miles farther. For the greater part of the distance the road is hilly, and in some places exceedingly steep. The views gained on the road, however, are fine. One sight alone, the mountains seen from the Saddle of Sargent, three miles from Bar Harbor, will repay the journey.

The village of Bar Harbor, concerning which nothing in particular has yet been said, is beautifully situated within a short walk of the beach, and close to Newport and Green Mountains—here our ever-present companions. In front are the Porcupine Islands, lying in the mouth of Frenchman's Bay, and beyond are the Goldsborough Hills. The prospect is not altogether unlike that found in some places on the shore of Lake Winnepesauke, and we do not always realize that we are looking upon salt water, until we catch a glimpse of some craft peculiar to the sea.

A beach extends along the front of the village on both sides of the landing. Here is fine bathing for those who like the cool temperature of the water, while the geologist will be delighted by the glacial marks deeply cut on the surface of the rocks.

Bar Island is the nearest of the Porcupine group, and twice in every twenty-four hours the narrow strip of sand connecting it with the main is uncovered, as if for the convenience of visitors, who can thus, like the Israelites, walk dry-shod through the sea.

This place will be visited first by those who are resolutely bent on seeing the whole island; afterwards the " Ovens " claim attention.

The Ovens are situated about six or seven miles northward, and it would not be profitable to go the whole way following the line of the beach, on account of the difficulties that are met, and the projecting points of land that double the distance. Going by the

beach it will be best to make Hull's Cove—two miles
—the first point, taking Duck Brook Cove on the way.
At high water a part of the way must be travelled
along the rocks. In some places they are quite high
and fringed with trees.

Hull's Cove is a very pretty place, shaped like a
horse-shoe, and has a sandy beach. There are only a
few houses. It was named after a brother of the
General Hull who was *not* shot for his cowardice at
Detroit, as the court decreed. Here dwelt Madame
Marie Therese de Gregoire, a descendant of De la
Motte Condillac.[1]

It appears that in the year 1688 the king of France
gave to Condilkac a large tract of land on the main,
together with the Island of Mount Desert, of which
he took nominal possession, and executed several
papers, in which he styled himself " Lord of Donaquee

(1)—In the petition of Madame Gregoire, her grandfather's name
is spelled Condillac. Elsewhere he appears as " Antoine de la Mothe
Cadillac, Lord of Bonaguat and Mount desert in Maine." He was a
native of Gascony. In the Paris Document (N. York Col. Doc., Vol.
ix. p. 591,) he is spoken of, under date of 1694, as " Sieur Delamotte-
Cadillac, Captain of a detachment of Marines, a man of very distinguished merit." In 1694—7, he commanded at Michilimakinac. In
1701 he established Fort Ponchartrain, Detroit, remaining with his
wife until 1703. The next year he returned to Quebec. In 1712 he
was appointed Governor of Louisiana. In company with de Crozet,
he controlled the trade and opened a silver mine. He returned to
France, March 9, 1717; and it is said by du Pratz (*Histoire de la
Louisiana,* Vol. i. p. 23,) that he died within two years afterwards.
He is identified with the early history of five or six States. The Paris
Documents, (N. York Col. Doc., Vol. ix. p. 446) say that he was well
acquainted with the New England coast; but his connection with
Mount Desert was nominal.

and Mount Desert." Donaquee was the Indian name of Union River, which empties into Blue Hill Bay. And in November of 1786, Madame Marie Therese de Gregoire, in company with her husband, Barthelemy de Gregoire, landed in this country from France, and appeared before the General Court at Boston, petitioning for the confirmation of her right, as the granddaughter of Condillac. In this course she was encouraged by Thomas Jefferson, La Fayette, and others. The court heard and granted her plea, July 6, 1787, and afterwards, by a special act, naturalized Madame and her husband, together with their children, Pierre, Nicholas and Marie.

In 1762 the General Court had granted the island to Governor Bernard, and the king had sanctioned the act, but his course during the revolution was obnoxious, and the island was forfeited. June 23, 1785, the court had also granted one-half of the island to Sir John Bernard, who had been friendly to the patriots; and the following December he agreed to pay two thousand five hundred pounds for the other half, but the contract was ultimately relinquished, and thus the Gregoires, as stated, obtained their rights. The vote, however, was intended to be a compliment to France, "to cultivate a mutual confidence and union between the subjects of His Most Christian Majesty and the citizens of this State.[1]

(1) — See Resolves of Mass., Vol. v. pp. 32, 131, 1789; Laws of Mass., Vol. i. p. 652, 1787; Papers Amer. Statistical Society, Vol. i. p. 76.

Madame Gregoire thus came into possession of about sixty thousand acres, embracing parts of the main land, and the entire island, except where already occupied by actual settlers.

On their advent at Mount Desert they began to sell off the land at a dollar an acre, but they do not appear, on the whole, to have been in very affluent circumstances. An old man at work in a field told me that he knew them well, and remembered the circumstances attending their death. Monsieur died first, after which Madame lived three years in the family of the Hulls, who occupied a house that stood on the site of the present brick one near the shore. After her death a belt full of gold was found on her body. About three-fourths of a mile back from the beach, the cellar of the Gregoire house is pointed out. Here, with their sea-side neighbors they lived a secluded life, dwelling upon the great memories of regal France. The old man, above referred to, said that they were occasionally visited by a French Friar; and that when Monsieur left home he usually went to lay in an equal stock of rum and molasses. Not, however, that he loved the sparkling vintages of Languedoc less, but Santa Cruz more. And too many of our sea-side friends are still overmatched by the same infirmity. At least the smugglers say so. At the cove, the antiquarian may give half an hour to digging among the Indian shell heaps, where perhaps he may find a stone hatchet.

Here it is best to leave the beach and follow the road until the burying ground is passed, and then strike across the fields of Point Levi to Saulsbury Cove. In going this way it will prove interesting to visit the graves of the Gregoires, found just outside of the burying-ground, at the south-east corner. We may rest assured that the Roman faith of the Gregoires had nothing to do with this exclusion. The grounds were laid out long after the Gregoires died, and, there being no monument, the graves were probably overlooked when the fence was put up. The interest that has been felt of late years in everything relating to Mount Desert has brought many visitors to the spot, now marked only by rude stones, but which, if we regard the interests of history alone, should at least be covered by a suitable monument.

The walk across Point Levi in a pleasant day is perfectly lovely. The woods and the fields are of the finest, while with what shall we compare the blue waters of Frenchman's Bay? The day we went to the Ovens the haymakers were at work, and the new-mown grass vied with the wild rose in delicious perfume, while the little folk we had along with us vied with one another in blackening their mouths with the ripe berries, afterwards pattering down to the cove, bearing long branches loaded with the fruit, like victorious palms.

Here we found our boatmen, who had come around

the point to meet us and carry us on by water, about two miles farther to the Ovens.

In going thither, always plan so as to reach the ground two hours after the ebb. The Ovens are nothing less than some fine caves in the cliffs which, being formed of a sort of porphyritic rock, is easily disintegrated by the frost and waves. The result is quite imposing. When the tide is part way down, a boat can be rowed under the largest. At low water a clean, beautiful pebbly beach is stretched along in front. The roofs and sides of the Ovens, when dripping with brine, present a variety of rich colors, combining with the rare lustre of the feldspar. The action of the weather is also slowly decomposing the surface of the rock all around on the top of the Ovens. A break in the cliffs affords a shelter for boats, and at the same time a place easy of ascent. Here come pic-nic parties innumerable.

South of the Ovens the cliffs are high and perpendicular. In a projecting spur is a long passage, through which it is deemed proper to pass. Some call it *Via Mala*, yet most persons are content to know it as The Hole in the Rock. Half-way up the cliff the harebells bloom in security, and here and there a miniature pine grows green in some rift.

A pleasant day here is always short, and the row back enables one to gain fresh views of the whole region that has been travelled on foot.

The next ramble should be southward to Cromwell's

Cove and the Assyrian's Head. The distance by
the shore is perhaps a long mile, though by the
road less. Starting from the steamboat landing, at
low tide the whole distance can be done below high-
water mark. Those interested in collecting pebbles
will find some good ones, though there is nothing rare.
Opposite Mr. Hardy's handsome cottage is an isolated
rock. Every one must climb this, because, forsooth,
it is Pulpit Rock. In some great cathedral, it would
serve a good turn for the preacher. All along in this
vicinity the schisty rocks are splitting up, showing
signs of stratification, while huge boulders, brought
hither by the Pre-Adamite drift, are seen struggling
with the noisy surf. This ramble affords a fine view
of the cliffs in one of the Porcupine Islands known
as Wheeler's. The reason for the name now also
appears, which is found in their resemblance to the
back of the animal bearing that name. The likeness
is not so apparent as formerly, for the reason that
they have lost so many of their dead trees, which
once stood as thick the quills of the "fretful porcupine."

At Cromwell's Cove there are fine studies in rock,
but here on the shore further progress is impossible,
the beach running down under the sea, which rolls
in against a perpendicular wall. Getting at the right
angle, a rock-man will readily be discovered, sitting on
a pedestal half-way up the cliff. The peculiar cast of
the features led to the name of "The Assyrian." He

only needs a little more strength in his nose to appear a model man.

Near the Assyrian is a fine rift, forming a sort of cave, into which the sea squeezes itself with no little force and noise. An ascending path runs along the edge of the cliffs among the trees, affording an outlook upon the boiling waters below.

This ramble will consume a whole morning, and, in returning by the road, a turn through the fields near the Connor farm-house will afford a glimpse of the " Footprint" in a rock. I first heard of this through the medium of a magazine called *The Maine Light*, which lived through one number and then went out in darkness. The editor, in setting forth the attractions of Mount Desert, speaks of impressions of human feet found in the rocks here and in the neighboring isles. An inquiry among the inhabitants brought this to light. It has long been known as the Indian's Foot. It is about fourteen inches long and two deep, presenting what appears to be the impress of a very tolerable foot. It is, no doubt, nothing more than a very curious fracture in a metamorphic rock. Persons passing that way will of course go and see it. The children of the ilk will be glad to earn a dime in pointing out the exact spot.

In crossing the fields from the Indian's Foot to the road, that somewhat rare flower, the purple orchis, may be found on a piece of lowland. It is of peculiar interest, the reader will remember, from the fact that Darwin brings it in to help his theory of Original Selection, by proving the fructification of the orchis by insects.

Next in order is Schooner Head, three miles beyond the Assyrian. This must be reached by the road, as between these two points there is an unbroken granite wall rising up straight from the sea. The walk to Schooner Head, like all these walks, abounds with interest. It runs along the eastern side of Newport Mountain, whose hoary cliffs look down in such solemn grandeur, and comes out through a fine grove of birches to the head of a cove. Schooner Head is a noble cliff close by the entrance of this cove. It is probably not so high as the next headland northward, but all things combine to make it more attractive. It takes its name from the fact that on its sea-face there is a mass of white rock which, when viewed at the proper distance, presents the appearance of a small schooner. Indeed, there is a tradition that in the war of 1812 a British frigate sailing by, ran in and fired upon it, the captain thinking it was an American vessel. This is not at all unlikely, for one day when approaching the coast in a steamer, my attention was directed to that " little vessel sailing so close to the cliffs." This was at least a very good vindication of the name.

Here is to be found what is known as the Spouting Horn. It is a broad chasm in the cliff opening part way down to the water on the east, with a low arch-way on the south side at the bottom communicating with the sea. At low water there is a slippery and dangerous descent to the arch, through which it is possible to pass, and then climb fifty or sixty feet, escaping from this horrible place at the top. When the tide is rising, the waves drive in through the arch, with great fury; and in severe storms the force is such as to send up the water above the mouth, spouting like an Icelandic geyser.

This is a place where in climbing every one should move with the greatest caution; for woe to the hapless wight who slips when crawling through the dark and slimy arch. The boiling surf will suck him down into depths from whence he would never rise. The climb has its grim attractions, and young ladies even sometimes go through the Horn; yet most persons conclude that it is better to keep in a safe seat and watch the billowy sea.

A fine day is generally given to these rambles, but stormy weather is the best. At such times there is a wierd attraction about the sea-side. Button up your rubber coat, therefore, to the chin, tie on a tarpaulin, and go forth with your staff, breasting the storm. The investment will be found to pay. The lush of gently-falling waves is fine, but what is this compared with the sea in a storm, telling its angry thought to these mighty cliffs, and pouring all its wrath against their granite sides? The memory of such a day is enduring. Many an odd character is also met in these driving storms. Whichever way the gale may come it always sends such to the shore. Besides, there is ever a chance of a wreck, or at least of a hair-breadth escape. How fine is the spectacle of a ship struggling on a lee shore, and how terrible when it becomes apparent that Death is on board. Sometimes one may lend a helping hand, while often he finds himself in need of aid.

In the cove the fishermen have their boat-houses, and from thence that go forth to set their nets and trawls. At one of their huts was a shark's back-bone fourteen feet long, drying in the sun. Passing around this place, along southward of the cove, we come to the Mermaid's Cave, an enormous den formed by projecting ledges. Two or three hundred persons could here find room. At high water the waves go thundering in to its farthest recess. It is the truest cave on the island, and besides it contains the finest aquarium mortal ever beheld. Here is a wealth of anemones that Cræsus and Dives could not buy. They appear in all the richest hues in their rock-pool parlors, floored with a hard, limy substance, in color a delicate pink. Transferred to New York, it would prove of fabulous value. But this an institution that cannot flourish in the full light of day. It prospers best in the shady "caves and womby vaultages." Near the edge of the cave, where the sunlight strikes, the pools were without an inhabitant; yet where the light was properly adapted, the colony was numerous. Here these exquisite creatures, resembling some rare flower, live and die without moving from the spot to which they are attached. They do not seem to know any fear, and are as willing to be fed as a chicken, though when you put your finger in their cup-like mouths, they will fasten upon it with their tentacles. Their homes are exquisitely fitted up with a variety of delicately-fronded moss of all colors, with sea lettuce and pale green sponge.

It would prove unfortunate, however, to be caught here by the tide ; and at the flood, as the waves come rolling towards the entrance, they often give a start, those who likened the cave to the home of Polyphemus now thinking that they

> " See Cyclops stalk from rock to rock,
> And tremble at their footsteps' shock."

Accordingly they leave its splendid pools and get out as fast as possible.

Our next ramble is to Great Head, the finest headland on the island, and the highest, it has been said, between Cape Cod and New Brunswick. It lies a short mile beyond Schooner Head, and is reached by the same road. Approaching the Head, we have a fine view of Newport's southern end descending to plunge into the sea. High up on the ledges are the nibbling sheep, foraging among the closely-cropped grass. Reaching the farm-house, most persons here leave their carriages, though the road extends some distance farther into the woods. The way is perfectly plain. The left-hand track leads by a gradual ascent directly to the Head. The woods are here and there largely sprinkled with fine old birches. Arriving at the highest point, a view is had far and wide of the grand old ocean, while landward rise the mountains.

This whole peninsula recently became the property of a Philadelphia family that has a taste for landed trifles. Among their effects, it is said, is an islet in Lake Superior, and a snow-peak in the Swiss Alps. But Great Head need not feel ashamed of itself in any company.

In one place there is a rough and steep descent nearly to the water, while in another a sheer wall leans forward, threateningly, over the sea. By descending the former a fine view of the face of the cliff is had; while a little way west, just below the gulch sprinkled with white rocks, is a cyclopean den called Stag Cave, from the resemblance to a stag which the imagination may easily conjure up when looking steadily upon some intrusions of milky quartz in the side of the wall.

Visitors are fond of coming to Great Head again and again to spend the whole day in sauntering from point to point, catching each new expression of the cliffs; or, book in hand, bestowing themselves under some convenient rock, to keep one eye on the stereotyped page and the other on the changeful deep.

Another fine ramble is to Otter Creek Cliffs on the ocean side of the tongue of land which makes the creek. The otter formerly abounded there, and hence the name. A separate journey can be made to this place by the way of Echo Notch, or else when at Great Head it may be reached by crossing the sandy beach on the west side. The specialty at Otter Creek is the cliffs, which are high, rugged and fine. There is moreover a cave called Thunder Cave. Following these cliffs down to the end, the creek may be crossed in a boat, and then come fresh beach rambles to North-east Harbor and the mouth of Somes' Sound, out of which, Agassiz says, when Mount Desert was " a miniature Spitzbergen," the " colossal icebergs " floated off into the Atlantic, " as they do now-a-days from Magdelena Bay."

Having reached this point in beach rambling it will perhaps hardly be profitable to return by the same route. It will be better to take the North-east Harbor road to Somesville, and thence, by the Mount Desert road return home.

The Falls

**SULLIVAN**

Skilling River

Hancock

44° 30'

Hog I.

Jones' Cove

Calf I.

West Gouldsborough

The Narrows

Lamoine

**FRENCHMAN'S BAY**

The Ovens

Salisbury Cove

Stave I.

Hull's Cove

44° 25'

Sheep

Bar Island Porcupine

Long Porcupine

Jordan's I.

**BAR HARBOR**

Round or Wheeler's Porcupine

Bald Porcupine

The Anvil

Winter Harbor

The Anvil

Egg Rock.

Spouting Horn

Schooner Head

Otter Creek

Great Head

Schoodic Point

44° 20'

Otter Cliff

Schoodic I.

# FRENCHMAN'S BAY.

## CHAPTER X.

D'AUBRI — THE PILLARS OF HERCULES — BOATING — THE ISLANDS — SHELL-HEAPS — ANTIQUITIES — MOOSE.

RENCHMAN'S Bay might perhaps be easily disposed of, by saying that here there *is* no Frenchman's Bay; and yet this would hardly prove a just proceeding. Besides, a multitude of witnesses who have loitered on its margin and tossed on its waves would rise up and declare me an imposter; yet, soft and fair, gentle Mount Deserter, for there is nevertheless somewhat to say.

The common story runs, as Williamson reports it in his History of Maine, that the name of French-man's Bay was given to these waters, for the reason that a French ecclesiastic, Nicholas d'Aubri, was lost here on an island. He refers to Sullivan, who tells the story with the important difference that he locates the scene on the west side of the Bay of Fundy, which Champlain says was named Frenchman's Bay by De Monts, though not on account of d'Aubri's adventure. This happened on Long Island, on the

east side of the Bay of Fundy. At a[1] somewhat early
date the original name appears to have been lost sight
of. It was afterwards revived, and applied to the
wrong place, the story of d'Aubri being imported to

(1) — Williamson, in his confused statement, refers for an authority
to Sullivan, and Sullivan refers to Abbe Raynal and Cartier, neither
of whom say anything about it. The Abbe (Vol. V. p. 344, Eng. Ed.
1798) simply mentions the fact that the present Bay of Fundy was first
called Frenchman's Bay. In truth there is no authority for the notion
that the bay received its name from the adventure of d'Aubri. Champlain in his Voyages (Paris Ed. 1613, pp. 13, 19) distinctly says that
the bay was named by De Monts. He briefly mentions the affair of
d'Aubri, but his language, as in the case of Lescarbot, shows that the
bay was known as "*la grande baye Francoise,*" before the adventure took place. The account of d'Aubri has been so poorly stated,
that it may be well here to give the version of Lescarbot, in the language of Erondelle, whose translation is now so rare :

"Hauing soiorned there some 12 or 13 daies, a strange accident
hapned, such as I will tell you. There was a certain [Roman] Church-
man of a good familie in Paris, that had a desire to performe the
voyage with *Monsieur De Monts*, and that against the liking of his
friends, who sent expressly to *Honfleur* to diuert him therof, and to
bring him backe to Paris. The Ships lying at anker in the said Baye
of *Saint Marie*, he put himself in company with some that went to
sport themselues in the woods. It came to passe that hauing staied to
drinke at a brooke, hee forgat there his sword and followed on his
way with his companie : which when hee perceiued hee returned
backe to seeke it : but hauing found it, forgetful from what part he
came, and not considering whether he should go East or West, or otherwise (for there was no path) he took his way quite contrarie, turning his backe from his companie, and so long trauelled that he found
himselfe at the seashoare, where no ships were to be seen (for they
were at the other side of a nooke of land farre reaching into the sea),
he imagined he was forsaken, and began to bewaile his fortune vpon
a rocke. The night being come, euery one being retired, he is found
wanting : hee was asked for of those who had beene in the woods,
they report in what maner he departed from them, and that since
they had no newes of him. Whereupon a Protestant was charged to

Mount Desert at the same time. We might therefore
be excused for saying that here there is, properly, no
such thing as Frenchman's Bay. "Mount Desert
Bay" would perhaps be a more fitting name. The
statement of Sullivan that "there were, anciently,

haue killed him, because they quarrelled some times for matters of
Religion. Finally, they sounded a trumpet throu the forest, they
shot off the Canon diuers times, but in vaine: for the roaring of the
Sea, stronger than all that, did expell backe the sound of the said
Canons and trumpets. Two, three and foure daies passe, he appear-
eth not. In the meane while the time hastens to depart, so hauing
taried so long that he was then held for dead, they weighed ankers to
go further, and to see the depth of a bay that hath some 40 leagues
length, and 14 (yea 18) of bredth, which was named *La Baye Francoise,* or the French Baye."

Thus the poor wretch was abandoned to his fate, and finally the
ships went to St. Croix and prepared to spend the winter. But in
the meanwhile Champlain was "sent backe to the Bay of Saint Mary
with a Mine-finder that had been carried thither for to get some
mines of siluer and Iron." And it is related that as they crossed the
"French Baie, they entred into the said Baie of Saint *Marie,* by a narrow strait or passage, which is between the land of Port Royal and
an Island called the Long Isle: where after some abode the said *Aubri*
[the lost man] perceaved them and began with a feeble voice to call
as loud as he could; and for to help his voice he advised himself to
doe as *Ariadne* did heretofore to *Theseus,*

> *Candidaque imposui longæ velamina Virgæ,*
> *Scilicet oblitos admonitur a mei.*

For he put his handkercher, and his hat on a staues end, which made
him better to be knowen. For as one of them heard the voice, and
asked the rest of the companie, if it might be the said *Monsieur Aubri*
they mocked & laughed at it. Bvt after they had spied the mouing
of the handkercher and of the hat, then they began to think that it
might be hee. And coming neere, they knew perfectly it was himselfe, and tooke him in their Barke with great joy and contentment
the sixteenth day after he had lost himself."

many French settlements on that part of the bay, which is opposite to the banks of Mount Desert, as well as on the island itself," is a gratuitous assertion, which has no foundation in fact. The only ancient settlement of which we have any knowledge, was that of St. Savior, in 1613.

Still, what's in a name? If we were to send the name, "Frenchman's Bay," to the Bay of Fundy, where it belongs, these waters would not appear brighter nor the sky more blue. Therefore, while repudiating Williamson's stale story of d'Aubri, we we will take the present cognomen, *cum grano salis,* which is to say, with a little salt sprinkled on it.

Having now, as Mr. Oldstyle said, discharged "a duty to history," we may look about us and observe the characteristics of this body of water, which, in some respects, is finer than the waters around the outside of South-west Harbor.

Frenchman's Bay is about ten or twelve miles long and seven or eight wide. At its mouth is Schoodic Point, which rises as it retreats from the water, terminating in that barren peak known as Schoodic Mountain. According to the estimate of the Coast Survey it is four hundred and thirty-seven feet high. Its great compeer, Newport, stands opposite at the west side. Together they form the Pillars of Hercules at Mount Desert. Inside of Schoodic Point is Ironbound Island, while some distance to the north are the Goldsborough Mountains. Beyond is the town of Sullivan, and at the head of the bay is Trenton. Another reach of the bay extends in a northerly direction to receive the Skillings River, where at low tide there is a considerable fall. At high water a large vessel may safely descend, though not long since a schooner broke loose from above at about half-tide, and in shooting the fall rolled over and snapped off her masts. Towards the entrance of the bay, opposite Bar Harbor, lie the Porcupine Islands. Besides these there are no islands worth mentioning, except several that lie close to the eastern shore. Between Newport and Ironbound is the best fishing, while the sailing and boating are excellent everywhere.

Yachts of various sizes are always in readiness for a voyage, and every day they may be seen scudding to and fro. We frequently went in the Dolphin, a fine large sloop, with snowy sails, whose careful skipper had ploughed the deep for thirty years, and knew every inch of ground from Cape Cod to West Quoddy. With a stiff breeze it was a pleasure to see the Dolphin walk the water, bound, say, for the Ovens. In these little voyages we learned as much about the island as the bay, and at every hundred yards the former put on some new expression. A mile out from Bar Harbor it appeared in brave greenery, all the hills verdant to their summits, while up the bay towards the north, this character would gradually become lost, and finally in swinging around the shore the mountains themselves would disappear. It is, however, the more beautiful to bring them back again. At one point, near the Ovens, all that can be seen is the blue peak of Newport, but gradually the whole height comes forth, having a perfect pyramidal form. Then Green Mountain rises, and finally the distant ridge of Sargent comes in view; and when we sail in between Bar Island and Wheeler's Porcupine, Newport is no longer a blue filmy cloud, but appears before us in all its wild beauty.

There are many localities of especial interest around the bay. Each of the islands has some peculiar attraction. On Bar Island, already mentioned, may be had fine rambles and views of the mountains. The antiquarian can here find Indian shell-heaps that will repay the labor of investigation. From this place I brought away some arrow-heads dug out of the refuse of these aboriginal kitchens; also some teeth of the black bear, finely enamelled, together with part of the jaw. On the next island is an interesting fishing station, occupied in the summer by very intelligent and respectable people from Trenton. On the pretty little island adjoining, called the Thumb-Cap, is another station. Beyond is the Burnt Porcupine, while the last in the chain is the Great Porcupine. On this island, near the south side, there has been some search for Kidd's treasure in years past. The most delightful, however, to visit is Wheeler's. It is of great height, and affords the finest view of

Newport that is to be had from the bay, and which is a favorite view with artists. The cliffs in this island have often been sketched, and in the hands of a skilful painter are capable of great effect. Take a sunny day for a stroll here, and you will fix a picture in the memory that will endure.

Three or four years since a bear from the mainland swam over to this island, having a mind to try a little mutton. As it turned out, he did the sheep no harm; for the people discovered what was going on and translated Bruin into steaks. At present there are no bears on Mount Desert, though a man at Bar Harbor assured me positively that one lately followed him on the road near Duck Brook.

In order to see the cliffs to the best advantage, it will be necessary to row under them in a small boat. This is perfectly safe, even with a heavy swell running, if you have command of the oars. And when out it will be well to visit the other island cliffs, if possible, as they possess features worth studying.

The cliffs on the sea-side of Iron-bound require a special voyage, and sails will be better than oars. The cliffs here, as cliffs, are superior to those on the shores of Mount Desert, though inaccessible to ramblers. On the same trip, if the wind is fair, many persons run across to Schooner Head and go home by the way of the shore cliffs, the interest of which never wearies. Approaching Cromwell's Cove, running close in, the Assyrian may be distinctly seen, though arriving in front he mysteriously vanishes, and appears to sink into the wall.

One of the pleasant trips is that to Goldsborough, by which we gain a somewhat near view of its commanding hills. Here is a pretty harbor which is most easily entered at high water. The village has a pleasant aspect, but looks down sleepily from the hill-side. The entrance of the Dolphin with flying colors, brought only a single individual down to quay, besides a couple of fishermen—one a Chief Justice—who had been spending a day looking after the trout. Their basket was so well filled with fine fish that one hardly need to fear recommending the waters of this vicinage to those who may be piscatorially inclined. At Goldsborough, however, the chief interest gathers around the shell-heaps, the relics of multitudinous dinners eaten during the old times by the Indians who dwelt around the harbor. These shell-heaps are often several feet deep, and sometimes cover acres of ground. They are mixed more or less with earth and ashes, and contain antiquities such as arrow-heads, stone hatchets and chisels, together with pieces of rude pottery, and the bones of birds and animals that were used as food. At the mouth of the harbor, the banks on either side are whitened by them. A sort of clam-rake with long teeth is the best thing to use in turning over the shells. In heaps like these may be found the bones of the moose, the deer and the bear, with those of birds. The smaller bones are sometimes worked into large needles or bodkins, of which the Indians often had need. These are all the memorials left by the once powerful race that ruled on these beautiful shores. Their arts were simple and few. In the Indian museums of New England, we find no sculptures to speak of that can be attributed to the Aborigines. I have seen on the handle of a pestle used to pound corn something that resembles the head of a snake, and in the collection at Harvard University, now being constantly added to by the zealous and well-directed labors of Professor Wyman, who has it in charge, there is a small image of stone. Perhaps this is the same that Whittier celebrates in one of his poems as a relic of the Northmen. This, with the exception of a fine amulet, carved in steatite, and found at Cape Cod, is the only sculpture of the human form that I have been able to trace to the natives on this part of the eastern coast.

Among the remains of birds found in the shell-heaps are a few of the bones of the Great Auk. One has recently been unearthed on this bay by Professor Wyman, to whom I am indebted for a sight of it. The Great Auk is now extinct, so far as these latitudes are concerned, and is only found in polar regions. There are now sixteen or eighteen specimens in European museums that must have been taken at a somewhat early date. The bones of the Auk tend to show that an arctic climate once prevailed here. At the same time the Esquimaux must also have extended down this coast. The Icelandic chronicles demonstrate, that in the eleventh century, a people called Skrællings, who possessed Esquimaux habits and characteristics, and sailed in skin-boats, were scattered along the shores of Massachusetts; and long ago they probably went northward in company with the Great Auk. We do not find any relics that can be distinctly attributed to them; yet occasionally the relics found even in these shell-heaps furnish hints of a people earlier than the Indians. Sewell, in his Ancient Dominion, is very positive, and after many investigations in connection with the heaps at Sagadahock and elsewhere on this coast, affording unusual relics, he says that the excavated rock-embedded kettle-bottoms "are the work of an earlier race than that which greeted Gosnold in these waters. These people," he adds, "were a sea-going people, skilled in navigating the deep in sailing vessels, sloop-rigged craft—and had vessels of copper for culinary use." What if these "sea-going people" were roving Northmen?

The bones most plenty in these heaps belong to the deer, but those of the moose are also found. We read in "A Brief Relation of the Discovery and Plantation of New England," bearing date of 1622, that in this new country there "is also a certain beast that the natives call a moose, he is as big bodied as an ox, headed like a fallow deer, with a broad palm, which he mues every year, as doth the deer, and neck like a red deer, with a short mane running down along the reins of his back, his hair is long like an elk, but esteemed to be better than that for the Saddler's use, he hath likewise a great bunch hanging down under his throat, and is of the color of the blacker sort of fallow deer, his legs are long, and his feet as big as the feet of our oxen, his tail is longer than the single of the deer, and reacheth almost down to his huxens, his skin maketh very good buff, and his flesh is excellent good food, which the natives use to jerkin and keep all the year to serve their turn, and so proves very serviceable for their use." After freeing his mind of this leaden paragraph, the old writer goes on to say : "There have been many of them seen in a great island upon the coast, called by our people Mount Mansell, [Mount Desert,] whither the Savages go at certain seasons to hunt them; the manner whereof is, by making of several fires; and setting the country with people, to force them into the Sea, to which they are naturally addicted, and then there are others that attend them in their boats with bows and weapons of several kinds, wherewith they slay and take at their pleasure." The writer concludes by declaring to his Royal Highness, Prince Charles, to whom the "Relation" is dedicated, that "there is hope that this kind of beasts may be made serviceable for ordinary labor with art and industry."

Such are the glimpses of Indian life preserved in the writings of that day. And in these shell-heaps are the remnants of their feasts. Cobbet, in the course

of his winter's captivity, may often have shivered over
the old hearth-stones that the antiquarian now digs
out.

The most accessible heaps from Bar Harbor are
those on Bar Island and at Hull's Cove, and all of
them require much patience and perseverance on the
part of the digger, as the relics are not so plenty as
some suppose ; though in the cart-track at the former
place I found a spot where the natives evidently made
their arrows, as the half-shaped fragments were dug
out all around it.    The stone used was a variety now
found near Katahdin, from whence some say it was
brought.    Going back to a period of three hundred
years we may imagine that a village of Red-skins are
here, and that still,

> " The old chief who never more
> May bend the bow or pull the oar,
> Smokes gravely in his wigwam door,
> Or slowly shapes with axe of stone,
> The arrow-head from flint and bone."

Yet this is only imagination.    The old chief has gone
forever.

# FOG AND ITS EFFECTS.

## CHAPTER XI.

The Air — Sunny France — The Gulf Stream — Fog — Leigh Hunt — Mist in Literature — Fog on the Mountains — Fog at Sea — The Phantom Ship.

COMPARATIVELY little has thus far been said about the atmosphere of Mount Desert. The most that has been written is the offspring of bright weather and fair skies. And yet there are two aspects of the case that should be considered in a candid estimate of the attractions of such a place.

The great Constable of France asks of the English,

"Is not their climate foggy, raw?"

Others have plied the same query regarding Mount Desert. The answer is readily given. The coast of Maine is not the Azores, nor Cuba, nor Bermuda. In the winter the air is "raw" enough to suit an Icelander; yet in summer the visitor who goes with tolerable lungs will find it bracing and agreeable. The Dog-days are an institution altogether unknown. At Mount Desert the Canicula exists only in the almanac. The shrilly-breathing zephyrus is always piping from the ocean for the refreshment of man, the mosquitos cannot live, except in the woods, and thin clothing is at a discount.

Still it cannot be said that there is always a perfectly clear sky. Tell it not in Gath, publish it not in the streets of some consumptive Askelon; but we must confess that in this isle, with all its enchantments, we find fog. Yet the reader should not receive a wrong impression from the above remark, since so much depends upon impressions. For instance, we all have an impression that France is "Sunny France;" hence it is not easy to make men regard what Bishop Cheverus said as true, namely, that they have as many pleasant days in New England in the course of a year as among the hills of Lorraine and Languedoc. Yet it is nevertheless so; and the reader is warned against the influence of any such formula as "Foggy Maine," lest it should prove impossible to demonstrate the fact that the summer climate of Mount Desert is equal to the attractive average claimed for the entire region by the genial Bishop.

The Gulf Stream, flowing out of the great tropic reservoir, ploughs northward in its ancient track, attended by a thin, invisible vapor, which, when it feels the cold breath of the Arctic Sea, is condensed like the steam from the spout of a teakettle, and rolls heavily away from the fishing Banks of Newfoundland in the form of confirmed fog, sometimes drenching every hill-top and valley along the coast. Mount Desert only gets its due share; and so far from being an objection, it adds to the beauty of the place, often throwing an ineffable mystery and charm over the entire island. Indeed, what would artists do without it? How well it hides a deformity or heightens an effect, let Landseer tell us in pictures of mountain scenery.

Whoever wishes to become an admirer of fog, should read Leigh Hunt's Essay. In his own charming way, he gives us the literature of the subject, showing the splendid use that Ossian makes of it, how Homer and Virgil introduce their gods and goddesses wreathed in its glories, and how Jupiter shrouded the Vale of Tempe with fog to hide his amour with Io.

It is to be confessed that Shakspeare was not in love with England's fog, yet Leigh Hunt goes into ecstacies over its effect when charged upon of an evening by the gaslight in London streets, an effect which he thinks worth mentioning in connection with the fine idea of Rhodius, who, after bewildering the Argonauts in the fog, brings down Apollo with his bow, in answer to their prayer, to shoot a guiding light before them to the nearest isle.

Here, and everywhere, it forms an element of sublimity, as well as of beauty. We had climbed one day to the top of Green Mountain to view the splendid panorama of land and sea offered to the eye,

> " When suddainly a grosse fog overspread
> With his dull vapor all that desert has,
> And heaven's chearcful face enveloped,
> That all things one, and one as nothing was,
> And this great universe seemed one confused mass."

I saw something similar to this once when looking
down from Mount Washington into Tuckerman's
Ravine, where the dense fog was tossed and rolled by
fitful gusts, giving the appearance of a boiling ocean.

At Mount Desert we have an opportunity of studying every variety of foggy display. Some days, it is
to be confessed, we found these vapory veils a sad
annoyance. It was unpleasant when we had arranged
the night previous for a tramp to Newport and a day
of rare enjoyment, to look out of our windows in the
morning and find that

> " aloft on the mountains
> Sea-fogs pitched their tents, and mists from the mighty Atlantic."

Our friend Aureole, who has already been frequently mentioned, and who occasionally indulged in
a transcendentalism, told us on one occasion as we
stood grumbling on the piazza, that our experience
was not at all singular, as half the people in the world
were in the fog all the time.

Yet in due season the advancing day often trans-
muted the cause of our wretchedness and discontent
into pure poetry; and then, when tramping through
Echo Notch, on the way to Jordan's Pond or Otter
Creek, Choriambus would call us to

> " Look down that dark ravine,
> And watch the white and swiftly-climbing mist,
> Rolling in silence up the narrow fissure
> Between those rugged, black, forbidding rocks,
> Like troops of angels climbing fearlessly
> Into a dark and rough and hardened soul;"

or else notify the less imaginative portion of the trampers of the all-important fact, that

> " From the hills
> White bridal veils of mist were lifted up
> By the gay sun, who kissed them till they blushed
> With light and joy,"—

a quotation particularly enjoyed by the young ladies.

We never failed to notice the fine illusions, nor neglect the mysterious antics played by the mist far out at sea. Here is where it is most effective in its exhibitions of magic. Sometimes, in a clear day, when not a sail can be seen in the whole offing, a great breath comes from the Grand Bank, spreading over the horizon a thin film of vapor, and suddenly a whole fleet appears sailing upon the sea. Whence come they? The philosopher tells us that a ray of light passing from a rare medium to a dense one, is bent downward; hence we always see the sun before he is really up. A slightly dissimilar operation of the light, reveals, perhaps, under favorable circumstances, a fleet of fishing vessels that is nearly out of sight below the horizon. Then with another puff of the breeze, the scene changes and this same fleet appears bravely sailing through the air. Again the fleet is doubled, one tier of vessels sailing over the other; or else, oddly enough, one tier bottom up, completely capsized—and yet securely sailing along the lower edge of a cloud, as the fly travels, feet upward, on a ceiling.   At the Isles of Shoals this effect is witnessed oftener than at Mount Desert.   Says Whittier :

> " Sometimes, in calms of closing day,
>     They watched the spectral mirage play,
> Saw low, far islands, looming tall and nigh,
> And ships, with upturned keels, sail like a sea the sky."

As for the effect of fog upon islands, we had a splendid illustration of it in crossing from Grand Menan to Lubec, when the Wolf islands, lying in the mouth of the Bay of Fundy, and which ordinarily, from that point, appear as mere specks in the horizon, now lifted up their fine rugged cliffs far above the surface of the sea.   In several cases the image was even trebled, so that three islands appeared one above another.   As on the real island there were a number of projecting points, these, in the beautiful economy of optics, were elongated into huge Doric pillars, upon which the two upper isles seemed firmly planted, the pillars being displayed between like the columns of a double gallery.   The sight was almost bewildering. The skipper said that he had often witnessed the same thing, but never saw a finer effect than this.

Leigh Hunt's admiration of London fog in the gaslight has been alluded to, and we may go back to the Isles of Shoals long enough to speak of a figure suggested in somewhat the same connection by Lowell, in a poem very unequal in its parts.   The poem referred to is descriptive of White Island and the vicinity, and suggests the resemblance between the huge beams that dart from the lantern into the mist and the arms of a giant reaching up towards the tower from the waves. He says :

> " And whenever the whole weight of ocean is thrown
>    Full and fair on White Island head,
>        A great mist jotun you will see,
>        Lifting himself up silently
>    High and huge, o'er the lighthouse top,
>    With hands of wavering mist outspread,
>        Groping after the little tower
>        That seems to shrink and shorten and cower,
>    Till the monster's arms of a sudden drop,
>        And silently and fruitlessly
>        He sinks again into the sea."

Tennyson also makes a good use of mist, and illustrates its capacity for scenic effect. In the Idyls of the King, describing the departure of Arthur from the convent, from whence he was seen by Guinevere, the poet says :

> " And even as he turn'd; and more and more
>    The moony vapor rolling round the King,
>    Who seem'd the phantom of a Giant in it,
>    Enwound him fold by fold, and made him gray
>    And grayer till himself became as mist
>    Before her, moving ghost-like to his doom."

A state of mind like that of the Queen's, would of course assist the illusion, yet both by sunlight and moonlight the effects of mist are often wierd and impressive in the highest degree, especially when they go so far in cheating our own senses. Hence comes the notion of the Flying Dutchman and the Phantom Ships in general, which find many a true believer

From Wolf-Neck and from Flying-Point,
  From island and from main,
From sheltered cove and tided creek,
  Shall glide the funeral train.
The dead-boat with the bearers four.
  The mourners at her stern,—
And one shall go the silent way
  Who shall no more return!

And men shall sigh, and women weep,
  Whose dear ones pale and pine,
And sadly over sunset seas
  Await the ghostly sign.
They know not that its sails are filled
  By pity's tender breath,
Nor see the Angel at the helm
  Who steers the Ship of Death!"

This, I believe, is quite an orthodox picture of the
Phantom Ship, which still occasionally sails into these
harbors, in foggy weather, to announce that some long
missing vessel has been buried in the deep. To deny
that the Phantom Ship was ever seen, would, in some
quarters at least, be denounced as heresy. Besides,
why need we doubt it? Sit on the rocks at Great
Head and watch, and you may see one of these unsub-
stantial craft almost any day. Talking about this
matter on one occasion among the cliffs at the above-
mentioned place, Mr. Oldstyle generalized the subject
somewhat after the style of Aureole, telling us that
it was not the fisherman alone who was led by phantoms ; that life itself was one long *mirage* and full of
unreal appearances shaped out of the fogs of the soul:
while the ever-ready Choriambus chimed in with a
Persian verse :

" From the mists of the Ocean of Truth in the skies,
  A *Mirage* in deluding reflections doth rise.
  There is naught but reality there to be seen,
  We have here but the lie of its vapory sheen."

As we rose up from our seat on the rocks, a strong breeze swept up from the south, dispelling all these weird illusions of the fog that hovered along the horizon, rolling away great fields of vapor, and leaving nothing before us but the open sea. Returning homeward, I heard Choriambus, who just then walked slightly apart, murmuring, half unconsciously, those well known lines from The Tempest:

" These *   *   *
*   *   *   *   *   *   *
Are melted into air, into thin air:
And, like the baseless fabric of this vision
The cloud-capp'd towers, the gorgeous palaces,
The solemn temples, the great globe itself:
Yea, all which inherit, shall dissolve,
And, like this insubstantial pageant faded,
Leave not a rack behind."

www.ingramcontent.com/pod-product-compliance
Lightning Source LLC
Chambersburg PA
CBHW030848270326
41928CB00008B/1274